"I'm Glad You Know Me!"

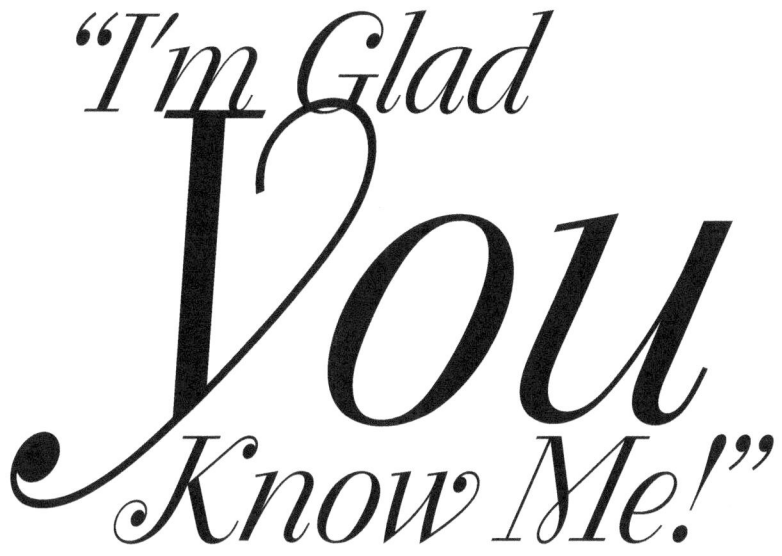

"I'm Glad You Know Me!"

A MEMOIR OF RELATIONSHIPS:
LOVE, FATE AND FORGIVENESS

Phyllis Barker-Pittman

"I'm Glad You Know Me!"
A MEMOIR OF RELATIONSHIPS: LOVE, FATE AND FORGIVENESS
Copyright © 2020 by Phyllis Barker-Pittman.

Matchstick Literary
331 Newman Springs Road,
New Jersey, 07701
1-888-306-8885
www.matchliterary.com
orders@matchliterary.com

All rights reserved. No part of this book may be reproduced or transmitted in any form or by any means, electronic or mechanical, including photocopying, recording, or by any information storage and retrieval system, without permission in writing from the copyright owner.

The views expressed in this work are solely those of the author and do not necessarily reflect the views of the publisher, and the publisher hereby disclaims any responsibility for them.

ISBN-978-1-6455-0856-4 (sc)
ISBN-978-1-6485-8678-1(e)

Library of Congress Control Number: 2015910346

DEDICATION

I dedicate this memoir to my dear loving and caring heavenly Father, God, and wonderful parents, Willie A. (Shag) and Burmia R. Hopkins-Barker. The very special ones who were responsible for my entrance into this amazing journey, called *"Life"*.

ACKNOWLEDGEMENTS

Much love, thanks and appreciation to all my special relatives and friends, who were some of the primary characters in this memoir. Special thanks to everyone who shared valuable information about me before I was born, and too young to remember. Because of their love, encouragement and support, I was able to compile all the information I needed to accurately complete this memoir, my 'testimony'. "I hope and pray this memoir will be an inspiration, encouragement and blessing to all who read it".

PREFACE

The desire for Phyllis to write this memoir dates back nearly four decades earlier, after experiencing several unpleasant and painful relationships, that began in the workplace. The experiences depressed her so deeply that her spirit was broken, left her wondering, if anyone cared. To soothe her pain, Phyllis began to write and vent, sharing her life experiences openly with the world, entitling the memoir, "Does Anyone Hear My Cry?", but never completed it!

Because Phyllis was blessed to live longer and experience life, while receiving many revelations, she realized she was not alone and was deeply inspired to change the title of this memoir to; "I'm Glad You Know Me!" **God** *ultimately heard her cry!*

After scarcely avoiding the first of three near death encounters and several very painful relationships, Phyllis later realized she was not alone, God was *always* present, watching-over, protecting and navigating her circumstances. Subsequently, allowing life to mold her character and find her purpose; *preparing her to be used by Him, for the good of humanity; His prized creation!*

During Phyllis' early childhood she was stricken with a serious near-death illness, hospitalized for an extended period and later discharged from the hospital to strict homecare for an additional extended period. While being ill and sheltered from play with her siblings and peers, Phyllis deeply missed and longed for their fun and loving relationship.

*"I'm Glad **You** Know Me!"* is intended to give *hope, restoration* and *healing* to those who have been broken; who are going, or has gone through painful, **unpleasant relationships,** *"Do not give-up,* **love**, *recognize your* **fate,** *and last, but certainly not least;* ***forgive!***"

INTRODUCTION

From Whence I Came…

My growing family of three, I wasn't born yet, 'a bun in the oven' soon to make my grand entrance into the world; 'humanities playground', along with a family friend who came along to help daddy with the long, tiring and tasking drive, migrating from the south to the north to find employment and a better way of life; scarcely avoided a devastating head-on highway collision. "Why on earth was my life, 'even before my birth' spared from such a horrific and terrifying tragedy, fatality?'

My mother, Burmia R. Hopkins-Barker was born in New Albany, Mississippi to the loving parents of Robert and Eula Morris-Hopkins. Momma was the fifth of nine children. She was the middle child, the 'pickle in the middle'. After momma's four older siblings left home, she became the eldest living at home. Her family lived and worked their own farm. Momma was very helpful to her mother on her multiple jobs; cooking, cleaning, baby sitting and working for the well-to-do families. She also helped her mother with bringing new babies into the world. Her mother was a very well-liked and trusted midwife in their community. Along with helping her mother, momma was also very helpful farming with her father. Momma later married my father at the age of fifteen. They remained in Mississippi for five years and added to their marriage union, two beautiful healthy children; a precious little girl and an adorable little boy. Sadly, and regretfully they lost their eldest little child, their precious little girl at the age of three.

My father, Willie A. Barker (Shag) was born in New Albany, Mississippi to the loving parents of Willie A. and Cora Deere-Barker. They were sharecroppers, living and working on their landowner's farm. Daddy was the eighth of nine children, and the second to the youngest son. Although daddy was not the eldest of his father's sons, he was named after his father because he looked so much like him.

Years later when daddy was twenty-two years old, he was drafted into the military, World War II and after serving his time in the army, he found employment right away, working as a Taxicab driver for a local cab company in New Albany. Being an army guy, a veteran, is probably what helped him to land the job so easily. Subsequently, daddy's job, driving cabs was a blessing to one of his older siblings'; his older brother and family who lived in Mercer, Tennessee. They were sharecroppers and tenants living and working on their landowner's farm, but they could never get from under the landowner's dishonest, unfair rules and agreements, leading them into a continual downward financial struggle, and always battling, trying to keep-up with his debts to his landowner.

Thankfully, daddy's job was his brother and family's way out from under the terrible, unfair clutches of sharecropping. The emotional stress, anguish and frustration of it all, forced daddy's brother into making a very important and serious decision, to leave Tennessee and move down to New Albany, Mississippi where daddy lived. Daddy and his brother secretly discussed and devised a plan for the move.

After daddy and his brother's secret discussion, his brother went down to New Albany, Mississippi and waited for daddy to bring his family down to him, as discussed. Daddy followed-up on their agreement and drove his cab up to Mercer, Tennessee during late night and picked-up his brother's family and drove them down to New Albany, Mississippi. Everything worked out beautifully, as planned! Thankfully, daddy's brother and family were no longer under the curse of sharecropping. Daddy was very thrilled and relieved that he was able to help his brother and family out of their terrible dilemma. Daddy soon married and started his own family, and five years later, he and his small family migrated up north to Racine, Wisconsin.

CONTENTS

Dedication		v
Acknowledgements		vii
Preface		ix
Introduction		xi
Chapter 1	Close Encounter of the First Kind!	1
Chapter 2	Close Encounter of the Second Kind!	5
Chapter 3	Discharged from Hospital to Homecare	11
Chapter 4	Given a Clean Bill of Health	15
Chapter 5	Family Purchases Our First Home	19
Chapter 6	Suddenly, "My World Came to A Complete Halt!"	27
Chapter 7	Returned to School after Giving Birth	35
Chapter 8	Introduced to My Sister's Boyfriend's Friend	37
Chapter 9	Proposed to While Still in High School	41
Chapter 10	Married, Senior Prom, and Graduation in '69	45
Chapter 11	Announcement of New Addition to our Family …Sad News of Husband's Draft into the Army	51
Chapter 12	The Celebration of Our Little Guy's First Birthday	55
Chapter 13	Husband Comes Home Before Deployment to VietNam	59
Chapter 14	Family Welcomes the Birth of Our Precious Baby Girl	63
Chapter 15	My Baby Girl Had A Bad Ear Infection	67
Chapter 16	Bad Sewage Forced Us Out!	71
Chapter 17	My Painful Experiences in the Workplace	73
Chapter 18	My Passion Left Me Broken!	81
Chapter 19	My New Birth	89
Chapter 20	My Unexpected Pregnancy!	93
Chapter 21	Close Encounter of the Third Kind!	97
Epilogue		101
Appendix		103

CHAPTER 1

Close Encounter of the First Kind!

It was September in the fall of nineteen fifty, during harvest time in Mississippi when my family of three and a family friend came along to help with the long, tasking and tiring drive; migrating from the south up to the north to Racine, Wisconsin for employment and a better way of life. I was not born yet, 'a bun in the oven' and due to make my grand entrance into the world next month.

Daddy started off driving for a while and became tired and our family friend took over. They switched seats; daddy sat in the front passenger seat. Momma, me, the bun in the oven, and my older brother sat comfortably in the back seat along with a few items. The adults were talking, laughing, and joking enjoying one another's company, but after a while conversation ceased, and laughter hushed.

In the quietness of the night and before dawning of early morning, the motionless, and scarcity of highway traffic, caused the ride to become very tiring, relaxing and calming, that deep sleep fell upon all the occupants, including the driver, and *suddenly*, momma awakens and yells, "*Shag, grab the wheel!*" Daddy immediately awakened, reached over grabbing the steering wheel, steering our car out of the way of an oncoming truck. Our friend had fallen fast asleep behind the wheel while our vehicle was veering over the center line heading head-on into an oncoming eighteen-wheeler truck.

Momma, daddy and our friend all realized the avoidance of that two-vehicle highway collision certainly was not by any means because of luck, or a coincident, that momma awakened when she did. The event was controlled by *fate*. My God intervened just in the nick of time and dispatched an angel to awaken momma, saving us from a devastating tragedy, a horrific fatality! An event that would have left no survivors; yes, even me, 'a bun in the oven', before I even had a chance to be born. My response to this encounter; "*Close encounter of the first kind!*" A supernatural event that if had not happened, would have changed the entire course of history; "*My amazing entry into life, My destiny!*"

Our family's first residence in Wisconsin was in a trailer court on the south east side of town in Racine, on Coolidge Avenue off Durand Avenue, where many families came migrating from the south for employment and a better life. Daddy's first job was at American Skein, a factory on Racine Street. The job paid well enough to provide for his growing family.

Well the big day finally came, October 2, my birth date, my grand entrance into the world, and our family suddenly grew into a family of four. My parents were happy to have a healthy baby girl, they had a complete family, two children, a boy and a girl. My brother wasn't alone anymore he gained a little sister and a playmate. Momma took good care of us and the house while daddy went off to work every day.

Time continued to pass, and our family had grown to five. I had another brother who was born one year and three days after me. When he was born, we were living on the north side of town on Michigan Blvd., we only lived there for a very brief period and moved back over on the south side to Mead Street.

"I'm Glad *You* Know Me!"

By nineteen fifty-five our family of six was living in the middle of the town, the "midtown area" on Metron Court. I was five years old then and had three siblings, one of which, was a baby sister, someone I could play and do-little girly things with.

My parents had friends that visited with us and sometimes would take my older brother and me to church with them on Sunday mornings. My younger siblings stayed home with my parents; they were too young to attend Sunday school. The church membership was small and met in the home of one of the member's family who lived on the south side on Ninth Street in Racine, but prior to the church meeting in their home, they met on Racine Street in the small home of one of their faithful female members, where the Church of Christ originally began to meet in the Wisconsin area.

Their minister commuted from Chicago to Racine for worship services and special church events. Subsequently, classes were taught, the word of God was preached and the membership began to grow, so much that the member's small house could no longer accommodate the rapid influx of new incoming members, and had to move into a larger home of another one of their faithful members, who also lived on Ninth Street.

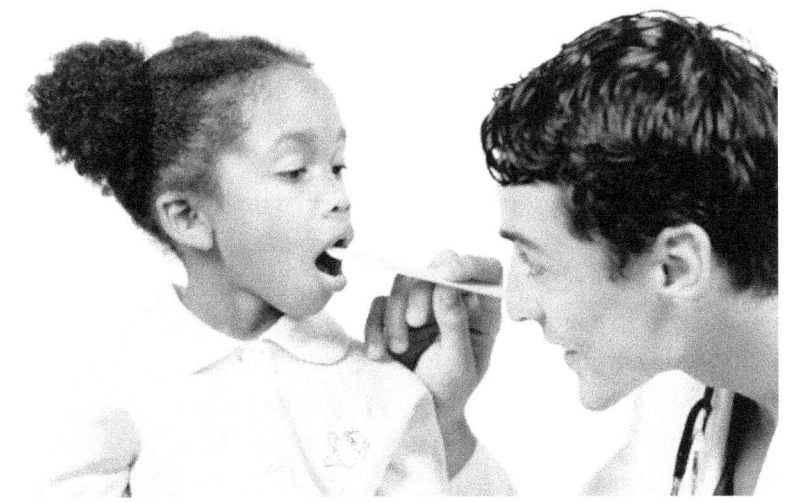

CHAPTER 2

Close Encounter of the Second Kind!

I t was nineteen fifty-seven and I was seven years old in the first grade and still living on Metron Court, across the street from the railroad tracks. I was a rough tom boy, an energetic little girl who loved playing and hanging with my brothers and their friends. We went to the railroad tracks to catch all kinds of small critters in our Mason jars. We caught beautiful butterflies, grasshoppers, grass snakes, lady bugs, and whatever else we could catch and fit into our jars. My younger sister stayed home close to momma playing house, little "girly" things with her baby dolls and stuff.

I usually played with my brothers and their friends when they came over. We'd head right across the street to the railroad tracks with our jars. We climbed trees, play with our marbles and did lots of fun things. Most of the time I was the only girl because my brother's friend's sisters were younger like my sister. I had no problem hanging with the boys. Every now and then, depending what we were doing outside, their younger sisters would join us. They were more girly like my younger sister, who enjoyed playing house and doing all the sissy things.

Well it happened, during the latter part of the summer when I suddenly was no longer able to keep up with the boys. I couldn't climb trees, run, and play and have fun with them. Before my illness, I enjoyed playing outside so much that I wouldn't let anything keep me from going out, even when I wasn't feeling my best. I wouldn't dare complain to momma because I was afraid, she would not let me go out to play. I would have to stay inside and do girly stuff with my little sister. But after a while momma did not have to make me stay inside.

My energy had left me, I was tired, my knees were achy and swollen, and all I did was lay around on the sofa. I did not have any energy or interest in being outside playing with the boys, or even inside playing with my little sister. After a while, momma noticed a change in my behavior and became very concerned especially because I showed no interest in going outside to play and was laying around the house. Momma's little energetic fun-loving tom boy was not at all herself. She first talked with daddy about what was going on with me, and they both agreed I needed to be seen by my doctor. Momma called my doctor's office, and she was told to bring me in to be seen right away.

After receiving a thorough examination and going through series of tests, my parents were given some very sad and terrible news. I was dealing with a combination of different illnesses that originated from a sore throat that, advanced into a strep infection caused by the streptococcus bacteria and advanced into rheumatic fever, a condition that often affects school age children, started from complications from prolonged, or inadequately treated strep throat that caused me to have fevers, soreness, pain and inflammation in my joints. It also caused me to be very tired, lethargic and low in energy. My condition had further advanced into rheumatic heart disease. My doctor heard a murmur in my heart. My heart was enlarged and very weak; all complications from a prolonged, untreated strep infection.

My pediatrician told momma and daddy my condition was so serious that I needed to be hospitalized immediately and receive surgery, but because of the serious condition of my heart I would never survive the surgery. He, in short was telling my parents, I was very near to death. His ultimate course of treatment for me, which according to what my doctor shared with my parents, was not even a guarantee; was for me to receive an antibiotic medication called penicillin in my veins, intravenously, an antibiotic used to destroy the streptococcus bacteria. Along with the medication, I had to be on strict bedrest with no play or activity, in a stress free and calm environment.

My pediatrician went on, telling my parents I would always have a murmur; I would never be able to play and lead a normal life or even be able to bear children. After hearing all the sad and depressing information about my serious condition, and the 'questionable effectiveness' of the medication (penicillin), momma was left with the understanding that the medication would either 'heal me or kill me'. In other words, if they gave me the medication and it didn't work, I could possibly die, but if they didn't even try it, and did nothing, *I would certainly die!*" It was a chance they had to take. Just the very thought of losing another child, their second daughter, desperately grieved their hearts. They prayed day and night that the medication would make me better, *"heal me!"*

During my hospitalization, in addition to being on strict bed rest, my treatment was also to be kept calm and quiet. If I needed to go to the bathroom, I had to be taken *via* wheelchair. All activities that caused physical exertion and excitability were totally restricted.

My total hospital stay was for three long months. All the hospital staff were very loving, kind and friendly. They made me feel special. When I was hungry during the night, they'd bring my special requests; buttered bread and chocolate milk. I often had someone come to visit and bring special treats and fun things; like long strings of assorted fruit flavored suckers, coloring books, story books, stuffed animals. Things that kept me quietly entertained.

The nursing staff, other departments and inter-disciplines in the hospital played a big part with spoiling me. The house keeping staff felt sorry for me because I was there for so long. They came in my room and stayed longer cleaning just to keep me company. The Nuns were nice too, they visited and brought treats.

Momma came as often as she could, but it was difficult because she had to get a ride and a sitter for my younger sister. It wasn't a problem with my brothers, they were at school. Momma was not driving and unfamiliar with the city transit system, so she either had to borrow a ride or wait until the evening, after daddy came home from work.

All the parents of my roommates were very nice. When they visited their sick child and brought them special treats and things, they usually made sure they included me. I was always sad when the time came for my roommates to go home, because I was being left behind. But the good thing was, each new roommate and their parents were as nice and friendly as the previous.

One afternoon while momma was visiting, one of my roommate's mother was visiting with her at the same time. Momma and her mother were just talking and laughing with each other, enjoying one another's company. I was very quiet, making no comments or responses. They suddenly stopped talking, and noticed me, that I was quiet, not saying anything. Well, I was just plain angry and being a brat, I was pouting. My roommate's mother asked me, with my back to them and holding my head down, "Phyllis, what's wrong honey?" With my lips poked out, looking like a cuddly little chocolate teddy bear myself, replied; "Why is her momma, (speaking of my roommate's mother), white and my momma black?" Momma and my roommate's mother were initially shocked, and speechless and couldn't say a word, but could no longer hold it in. They both looked at me and then one another and burst into laughter. They knew I was pouting. I was upset and jealous because they were not paying me, the spoiled little brat, any attention, and that, I truly was; a spoiled little brat! *"From the mouths of innocent babes!"*

My doctor continued to make regular hospital visits. He examined me thoroughly and kept my parents well informed of my condition, which continued to show more and more improvement as time went on. I became so much stronger and gained quite a bit of weight, because I was not physically active along with having a good appetite, and eating all my favorite night time snacks helped to put on a few pounds, along with the I.V medication penicillin, which also contributed to some of my weight gain, along with a culmination of strict bedrest, and an excellent appetite, caused me to be one chubby little lady. The odor of my medicine could be smelled through the pours of my skin. I reeked like medicine.

The time came, and my doctor had some amazing news for my parents. Yes, it was happening. My health had improved, and I was finally able to go home to be with my family. Momma was so happy and excited that she began to cry, giving all the glory to God, her Father, thanking Him for hearing and answering her continual prayers, and allowing me, through His loving care to recover from a serious, near death experience, a *'Close encounter of the second kind!'*

CHAPTER 3

Discharged from Hospital to Homecare

When I came home from the hospital a hospital bed and wheelchair were already there for me. The strange thing was, we were living in a different house from where we lived before I went into the hospital. Yes, we had moved once again, back to the Southside, on Franklin Street across the street from our school, Franklin Elementary & Jr. High School.

I was sad when my brothers went off to school every morning because I couldn't go with them. My little sister was not old enough to go to school yet, we quietly played together. We had fun coloring in our coloring books, watching cartoons and playing with our dolls. We were able to keep ourselves quietly entertained while our brothers were gone. Daily naps after lunch was a routine scheduled event for us girls. It was just so good to finally be back home with my family.

Daddy worked hard for our family. Momma was taking really good care of me. She was treating me nice just like the hospital staff. Catering to all my requests, wants and needs. She took me to the bathroom day and night as often as I asked. Some nights she just put me back into bed and I'd call for her again. The problem was, I was not that thin little frail girl that I was before I went into the hospital. I became a chubby little thing, not very light to lift in and out of the bed, back and forth into my wheelchair.

Well it happened one night. It was the straw that broke the camel's back. Momma finally came to the end of her rope. I guess you can say, I pushed my luck, yeah! I went too far! And before I knew it, she was spanking my behind. Momma was tired, she was just plain exhausted from all the lifting and taking me back and forth to the bathroom. Of course, I cried for a while, until I fell off to sleep. Momma felt sad for me, but she kept a close eye on me, checking on me throughout the night. Guess what? Momma did not have any more problems from that night on with me asking to go to the bathroom throughout the night.

After being home for a month momma took me to my doctor's appointment and told him what happened that one night. She had come to the end of her rope and spanked me because she was so tired and worn-out from not getting any rest. My doctor's observation was that I was okay and had survived the spanking, he was very pleased with my progress and how much I was improving. He chuckled, telling momma I was doing well and that he was sure she probably had taken all that she could, before going to that extent. He also told momma she was doing an excellent job taking care of me, such a good job that he asked her if she would be interested in becoming a licensed practical nurse (LPN) under his training. She refused the proposal because of having a young family at home, but she was also afraid to even try.

The time finally came after being hospitalized for three months to be discharged to home care for an additional three months, a total of six months, yes, a half of a year of medical care, and I was finally able to return to somewhat of a normal childhood. My doctor released me from home care to attend school, which was across the street from my house, because of my long-term illness and having missed so much school, I had to repeat first grade.

Although I was discharged from homecare to school, my doctor again gave orders and restrictions for my return to school. I had to continue to take oral antibiotic (penicillin). I could not participate in the physical activities of play or gymnastics. I had to sit and watch my classmates and not participate in their physical activities. I really didn't mind so much because I was just so happy to be able to be out and around my classmates. Gradually, as time went by, I made friends and build strong relationships, some became friends probably because they felt sorry for me, not being able to play and have fun with them. My teachers supervised me very closely, making sure my doctor's orders were being followed through.

A couple years later in 1959, our family moved into a different house on the other side of town, we were still renting but this time on the north side of town, on Randolph Street. We again moved across the street from a railroad track. I attended Jefferson elementary school. We didn't live very far from school. Some of our relatives and close friends lived in the area, or on the same block with us.

The physical restrictions in school continued but momma allowed me to go out for short periods to play low energy games like; Blue light, yellow light, red light "Stop light!" with the other kids. My doctor visits, check-ups continued regularly and at each visit he was very pleased with my progress.

One sunny day when I was outside with my brothers and their friends, at the home of the boys we played with before I became seriously ill, they were shooting marbles, and I was climbing a tree in front of their house. As I was climbing, I felt a strange presence, as if someone or something was looking down at me. I didn't understand who or what it was, but it really felt strange, as if I was being watched over.

While we were living on Randolph Street, momma taught herself how to cut guy's hair from experimenting on daddy and my brother's hair. She did so well she soon adventured into cutting most of the male's hair in our family. She also taught herself how to press and curl the lady's hair and put in finger waves from doing her own hair. The finger waves ended up being a signature talent for momma. Her waves usually lasted two-weeks, or until it was time to be done again. Momma enjoyed doing her hair and did an excellent job. She always kept her hair up and looking nice.

Momma soon ventured off into starting her own business as a barber and beautician. She started with her sister's and other female family members and friend's hair. When momma finished their hair, they were always very pleased and looked forward to their two-week return. Momma received so many compliments and did so well, that many of our relatives, friends and neighbors became momma's loyal customers. They all began to spread the word to their other relatives and friends. That was the beginning, yes, the start of momma's entrepreneurship. Her clientele was both guy's haircuts and females press and curls. She was doing so well that many of her new customers came from other beauticians in town.

Some Sundays our family would take a drive up to Milwaukee to visit momma's only aunt and family, my grandma, Momma Eula's older sister and her adult children. The daughter was a very successful Avon Representative. She often brought products for us when she visited.

One Sunday, as we were on our way up to Milwaukee to visit my aunt and family; daddy wanted to have fun with us kids. As we were passing by the Cemetery way out on Washington Ave., daddy asked us, "How many dead people are out there?" Of course, we all started guessing and throwing out lots of numbers. Daddy laughed and replied, "I hope they're all dead!" Oh boy! Did we ever get a big kick out that one? Momma, daddy and all of us laughed out heartily.

CHAPTER 4

Given a Clean Bill of Health

It was just before the start of a new school year and I was entering into the 7th grade at Franklin Jr. High, and due to be seen by my pediatrician for a complete physical before starting school. Momma took me to the doctor's office. It was a very long visit. He examined me thoroughly, he looked inside my mouth, at my throat, listened to my heart and lungs, and ran a series of tests. According to the all the results of my examination and tests, my pediatrician gave us some wonderful news; I was given, *A clean bill of health*. "Praise be to God". Once again, momma's prayers were answered!

Before discharging me from his care, my pediatrician gave momma some discharge orders and information. He told her I was no longer under any physical restrictions; I could participate in all physical activities along with my siblings, family and friends, but I would need to be pre-medicated with an antibiotic, penicillin, before having any dental work. My doctor also told momma to be sure to bring me in right away to be seen if I should develop any of the symptoms I had before my hospitalization. Yes, it was finally happening, and it truly had been a long time coming. Yes! it was all over, no more medicine, restrictions, "solitary confinement" or frequent doctor visits!

My junior high years were so much fun. I met lots of new friends. Some of who happened to live in my neighborhood. We went to school together and had sleep overs. I was so happy to be able to participate in fun and activities with my friends and classmates because I spent so many years sitting off on the sideline, watching while my classmates were having fun; running, jumping and playing nicely with one another. Unlike many of my classmates, I really enjoyed gym class a lot. It was so much fun being able to be involved in sports; to play on basketball, soft ball and volleyball teams.

I enjoyed school and did very well in school. Getting my homework done and keeping my grades up were always my top priorities. Beside attending school, I began babysitting for momma's younger siblings, other relatives and friend's children, and along with a couple other small jobs, which were beginning to keep me from being involved in some of my after-school activities.

One day when I was in junior high school, we students were changing classes and our teacher was not in the classroom when we arrived, so we were conversing and laughing with each other as students usually do when the teacher was not present. I guess we had gotten so loud and noisy that we didn't even notice our teacher had entered the classroom, yelling trying to get our attention, she used a few curse words. Before I knew it, I shockingly responded, saying, "You're fired!" She angrily looked at me and pointed her finger in the direction of the door and yelled, "Get out!" When we as students were told to leave the class, we were expected to go and stand out in the hallway next to our class and I did as I was told, and while standing, the principal noticed me and walked up to me, and asked me to come with him to his office, so I followed behind him. After arriving to his office, we sat down and he asked why I was not in class. I explained to him what had happened. He listened to what I had to say and sent me back to stand outside of my classroom until the end of the class or until my teacher gave me permission to return to class.

Well, when I returned to class the next day our teacher greeted us and apologized to the entire class for how she spoke to us and the way she handled the situation. All of us students thought it was nice of her. We did not hold any bad feeling against her, neither did she hold anything against us. I guess you can say; it was probably one of her "bad hair days". Thankfully the issue was easily resolved.

As for having problems with sore throats, (strep) infections, I continued to have occasional recurrences from time to time during my school years and continued to take the oral antibiotic, penicillin as previously, and at the earliest sign of any of the "familiar symptoms" momma immediately took me for medical attention. She got right on top of things each time and took me to see my doctor, which was a new doctor, a female gynecologist, who treated me with the same antibiotic, penicillin and also an additional order and instructions for treatment for my sore swollen throat; Hydrogen peroxide solution and warm water 1:1 gargle mixture. The treatment with the antibiotic and the gargles made all the difference in the world in minimizing both the soreness and swelling of my tonsils.

CHAPTER 5

Family Purchases Our First Home

1962 was a good year, momma was pregnant and expecting to have her baby in a couple months. I was twelve years old and our family of six just bought and moved into our first home, back over onto the south side of town on the corner of 13th and Highland Avenue. It was a nice two story one family home with three bedrooms upper and one bedroom lower, a nice size kitchen, a large living and dining room. The floors were beautiful hardwood that shined like a new penny. We moved next door to two nice families who lived in an upper and lower two-family home. The family that lived downstairs were related to the family upstairs. The family downstairs had two daughters. The oldest daughter and I shared the same name and we were the same age, but of a different race, white. Strange huh, I know!

Her father worked in the factory across the street from us. We girls went to school together had sleep overs and became the best of friends. Our families bonded well, and our relationship became very cohesive.

On May 10, we had a new addition to our family, a healthy little baby brother. When momma came home from the hospital with our little brother, our next-door neighbor came over to help. She was so very helpful to momma with caring for my baby brother and the whole family. She cared for us as if we were her own family.

Although we lived in the city, we had some farm animals in a fenced cage in our back yard. We had a rooster and some chickens to lay fresh eggs. The bad thing about it was, the rooster was our alarm clock. It woke us up early in the mornings from its crowing. The week-end mornings us kids liked to sleep in but that didn't happen very often. Between the rooster crowing, and daddy waking us up early for a hot breakfast, we were up earlier than we really wanted to be, but we found out, the breakfast was well worth getting up for, it was always very delicious!

When some of our friends from school came over to visit, they'd laughed and made fun of us for having farm animals in our back yard, like we were in the country. We enjoyed everything momma cooked when she used the fresh eggs from the chickens, they really made the best breakfast and homemade desserts. In fact, I learned how to bake delicious, mouthwatering "southern-style" three-layer cakes from scratch by observing and helping momma when she was in the kitchen baking.

Momma and her female siblings were all great cooks, that's because their momma was an excellent cook! When momma was a young girl growing up in the south, she and her momma, my grandmother, Momma Eula cooked and worked for a prominent family in New Albany. They absolutely loved her cooking and especially her baking. They loved Momma Eula's desserts so much that they convinced and entered her into several dessert bake-off contests, which she ended up winning first prize in most of the competitions.

Our family didn't have to wait for special occasions or holidays to have desserts. We had some type of dessert practically every day of the week. Daddy and us kids really enjoyed coming home to the aromas of the delicious smelling food, especially the desserts. Daddy even made his own special kind of desserts, white potato (Idaho, or Russet) pies and cobblers. They were desserts most people never even heard of and they were yummy!

Momma received lots of compliments on her delicious homemade desserts, and even had requests from family and friends to bake dessert for them to purchase. Subsequently, their requests influenced momma to start her own baking business in her home selling desserts. Her business went well. She baked for her niece and nephew who owned their own restaurant business on Racine Street. Everybody raved about how good momma's desserts were. She baked and sold different varieties of cakes and pies; Chocolate, cream caramel, pineapple, and coconut cakes. Chocolate, coconut, lemon meringue and sweet potato pies.

Daddy loved hamburgers and cheeseburgers, probably as much or more than Wimpy, the bald guy in the cartoon; Popeye the Sailor Man. Whenever daddy wanted hamburgers or cheeseburgers, he'd say to my sister or me, "Make me Wimpy". We got the biggest kick out of him. It was daddy's way of humoring us into cooking his burgers for him, of course it always worked. Daddy liked to have fun and laugh a lot. He didn't like seeing anyone being sad around him. He was always the life of the party. Daddy, being his age, was very agile and flexible. He entertained us kids and anyone else who were interested enough to stick around to see him doing all different kinds of unusual body movements, that his younger children couldn't even do. Amazing!

Daddy enjoyed hunting. He and my uncles had some hunting dogs, beagle hounds. He my older brother and uncles went rabbit, squirrel, pheasant and deer hunting. Daddy thought so much of his hunting dogs that he cooked the bones he got from the butcher at his part-time job, at the A&P supermarket up on the avenue. Although the bones had a little meat on them, I still thought it was *a little strange*, but the aroma from the broth cooking didn't smell bad at all, like people's food cooking. After dinner and before going down for his short nap and off to his part-time job, daddy normally left the bones on the stove cooking on low.

One evening while daddy was sleeping, he had the dog bones on cooking, my younger sister had her friends over. I had worked so hard, just finished cleaning the house. She went into the pots where the bones were cooking and dipped a large serving spoon into one of the pots of seasoned liquid broth and chased her friends throughout the house, dripping that yucky stuff all over my nice clean floors, making a big sloppy mess. I asked and pleaded for her to stop but she was having too much fun laughing and running through the house behind her friends. I was so upset with her I didn't know what to do. Momma wasn't home at the time. She left me cleaning and went visiting her sister around the block from us. I didn't really want to awaken daddy because he works so hard, but I couldn't get my sister to stop, so I went ahead anyway, tried and tried to wake daddy, but he wouldn't wake up. I then took things into my own hands, and yes, it ended in a big fight.

Yep! That did it. We awakened daddy, he heard all the commotion, my sister's big mouth yelling and crying, as if I was killing her. Of course, I was the one who got in trouble, "yeah, the whipping". I told daddy I tried and tried to wake him, but I couldn't get him to wake-up. Tearfully, I left home going through the back alley to my aunt's house where momma was. While crying, I explained everything to her about what had just happened, after I finished, we walked back home together. Once we made it home momma asked my sister's friends to leave. She talked with my sister first then gave her a good whipping. You're right, *she never tried that again!*

My younger brother, the one between my sister and me, was always being such a big nuisance to us. One time when daddy and the other guys went rabbit and squirrel hunting. After daddy was done skinning and cleaning them, my brother went back and got their tails and chased my sister all through the house with them; screaming and hollering, like she was crazy. He got such a big kick out of scaring her. But I was a "tom boy" and wasn't at all afraid of the tails, in fact I was laughing and enjoying all the excitement. I guess you can say she received her pay-back, for what she had done to her friends a while back, when she was chasing them through the house with the "yucky" broth from the bones daddy was cooking for his hunting dogs. I'd say, Karma is sweet!

"I'm Glad *You* Know Me!"

My older brother had his own boxing (speed bag) and weights he used and stored in our garage behind our house on Highland Ave., at the lower end of our fenced-in back yard. He had his own personal fitness club, where he worked out as often as he could. He was really committed to working out regularly by himself and with his friends when they came over. His friends often teased him about having a chicken coup with chickens and a rooster in our back yard. Yes, in the city! They called our family the "Beverly Hillbillies". We really enjoyed the chicken's fresh eggs for breakfast and momma loved using them for baking all her delicious desserts.

Ever since momma was a little girl, she's always wanted a piano, but never had the opportunity to have one. Later in life, as a wife and mother, her childhood dream finally came true. Momma purchased herself a beautiful Gordon Laughead Console Piano from the music store uptown on the Avenue. She started off taking piano lessons but soon stopped and began practicing on her own and taught herself to play by ear.

It was my younger brother who really grew into loving to play the piano and became very well at it. He did not take music lessons, he was self-taught, very dedicated and practiced a lot. My brother entertained our family and friends when they were over visiting. His playing the piano was often our main attraction.

Besides babysitting my baby brother when he became old enough, I earned money babysitting for the children of my momma's three younger siblings, nephews and nieces as well as other relatives and friends. I ironed and darned clothes for my aunt who had four children. According to my uncle, her husband, I would one day be an excellent wife and mother, because I gave such good care to their children and home when they left them in my care.

After a while, my income had grown, and later earned more money; pin curling and roller setting my upstairs neighbor's hair. The problem with babysitting was, I had to sit with my younger brother and on my jobs too, along with a couple other jobs, caused me to miss out on lots of fun with my friends and classmates, unless of course, I could talk one of my siblings into sitting with our baby brother, which usually came with a price. Yes, I had to pay!

As for my earnings, after a while I began doing so well from my combined jobs, I was able to start a small savings account. My bank was in a small secret hiding place in the back of our, me and my sister's huge walk-in closet. We shared closets, but I was the only one who knew my money was there. Earning my own money really felt good, having the opportunity to buy and do different things for myself, my family, and friends.

On the weekends when I wasn't working, I stayed home cleaning house, washing, hanging out laundry, and doing other household chores with momma. While we worked, we turned our work into fun; listening, singing and dancing to our favorite music on the record player and before we knew it, all our work was done!

One of my aunt's and her husband, the ones with the four children, along with their nephew and his wife, started and operated, as a partnership, A Rhythm and Blues Booking Agency, that lasted for a couple years in the mid-sixties called, "The Big Four," They booked several vocal artists and groups to come and perform in Racine at the Masonic Hall on the south side, on the corner of Dekoven and Mead street.

My sister and I had the awesome opportunity to attend a few of the amazing shows. Some of the R & B artists the partnership booked were; B.B. King, Betty Swan, Mary Wells, Tina Turner and The Jackson 5, just before they became famous. The Jackson 5 came to Racine after leaving a tour in Hawaii. They were wearing their lei when they came to perform for us that evening.

"I'm Glad *You* Know Me!"

When Michael Jackson saw me from the stage, he held his finger up beckoning me to the stage. After approaching the stage, he removed his lei from around his neck and took his beautiful purple colored lei, and placed it around my neck. Jackie, his brother, placed his gold colored lei around my sister's neck. We had a total blast that night, a night we'll never forget. We still have our lei until this day, a little frayed and considerably faded, but still intact. We have them safely stored away. *What wonderful memorabilia!*

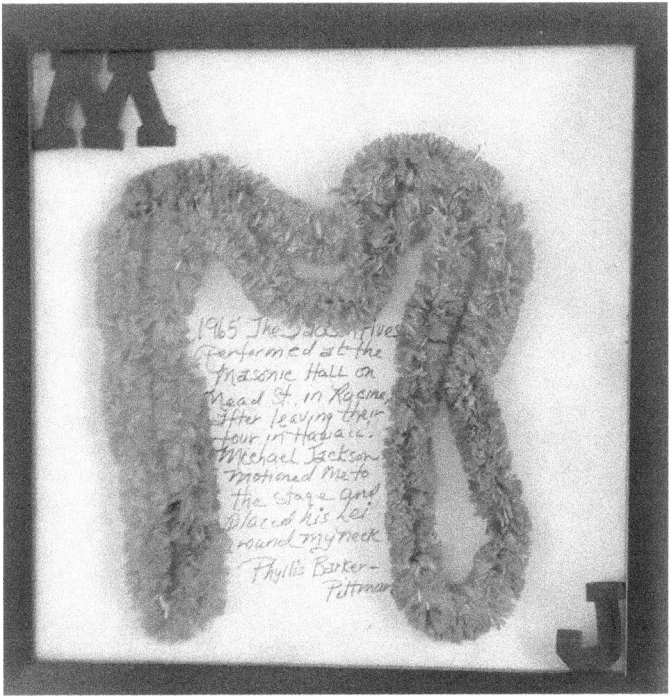

CHAPTER 6

Suddenly, "My World Came to A Complete Halt!"

We're still on the corner of 13th and Highland Avenue but we had different neighbors who moved next door into the upper and lower two family house. The families that we had a very close relationship with had moved away. The new family that moved in, was very large and needed both the upper and lower levels to accommodate their family size. They converted the two-family house into an upstairs and downstairs single-family home. Strangely enough, we later noticed, the new family happened to be one of our former neighbors between our frequent moves. But who would have ever thought our paths as close neighbors would ever cross again? Their family was not as large then but had grown considerably since we left them on Franklin Street. Our reunited family's sort of picked-up from where we left off, and even grew a closer and stronger bond. Although they were a large family, they always had plenty to eat, the children never went to bed hungry, and in fact they even had enough to feed their visiting friends and unexpected guests.

The mom was an excellent cook, I especially liked her delicious hot rice, raisin and biscuit pudding. I enjoyed making coffee for her and momma when she was over visiting. They spent lots of time together and became as close as sisters. They developed a mutual fondness for playing cards games, and having card parties, where my sister and I picked-up, and learned some choice cuss words, which we heard plenty of, while serving coffee and food to the card players. The card parties alternated between homes, which usually started on Friday evening and lasted throughout the entire weekend.

As for our new neighbors and old friends, I was the mom's favorite, and my sister was her husband's favorite. Their oldest child was a girl several years older than I. Her fiancé' was in the military. He came home on military leaves every so often to spend time with her. She was like an older sister that I never had the opportunity to know. My parents lost my older sister, Vivian when she was only three years old, before I was born. Momma often talked about how smart she was for her young age.

For special occasions I enjoyed helping my friend bake homemade cookies to send to her fiancé in the army. We baked lots of different varieties of delicious cookies. She also included me when she and her friends were going places and doing fun things. Her family and friends became my family and friends. Her family even invited us to their annual family picnic at Dandelion Park in Northern Wisconsin. My sister and I went a couple times and one time when we went, wore our pastel colored blue and pink floral print bell bottom pants and solid colored pastel pink or blue blouse. I wore the baby blue blouse and my sister wore the pastel pink. Of course, we thought we were looking good. We played all different kinds of fun games and ate lots of different varieties of good food, we had a blast!

One Saturday afternoon, my sister and I got ourselves into big trouble. Our nuisance brother did not give us a message that momma told him to give us, about not leaving home. She was next door at our neighbor's playing cards. My sister and I wanted to go out with our friend's joy riding for a couple hours, so we convinced our older brother to take care of our baby brother. Yes, you might know, our loving brother didn't give us the message.

"I'm Glad *You* Know Me!"

My sister, and I went for a ride with our friend's, listening to the music on the radio, sightseeing and watching people doing people things.

Surprisingly, when we came back home from our short city excursion, our brother was the very first person we saw, standing on the front porch, yelling at us as we were coming up the steps, "Y'all in trouble, y'all gonna get a woopin!" He went on to tell us momma was in the house waiting for us. After listening to him and telling us all that, my sister and I became very nervous, afraid and tearful, especially when we didn't really know why momma was so upset with us. Never-the-less, we went on into the house, *scared to death!* We left our brother on the porch laughing and snickering, knowing he didn't give us momma's message.

Of course, being the eldest, I got it first, yeah, the *'whipping'*. But, while waiting, my sister thought within her smart little mind, to do something quickly, but actually not very smart; to minimize the pain she was about to fore take, and taking advantage of her *"wait-time"*, she quickly ran upstairs to change from her Daisy Dukes to a pair of thicker slacks before momma got to her, of course, when it was her turn, momma noticed right away she had changed, causing her to be even more upset, and she gave her a whipping she'd never forget. You might know, our mean, spiteful brother was nearby while we were being disciplined, enjoying himself and having himself a laughing party. Our brother was truly *a major nuisance and a pain in our butts!*

In the fall, during the harvest seasons, momma and her sisters did lots of canning; fruits, vegetables etc. They also put lots of different foods in the freezer. Momma made the best homemade apple butter in the whole world. She had shelves and shelves lined up with all her delicious apple butter, jellies, preserves, beets, cabbage, green beans, mustard and collard greens, pickles, spaghetti sauce, etc. Daddy also stocked our freezer with all kinds of meats; beef, chicken and some of his hunted game. My parents made sure we had plenty to eat throughout our long cold winters.

Two of our neighbor's sons really loved momma's homemade apple butter a lot. Unbeknown to her, when it was my brother's, the nuisance's, turn to do the dishes, he paid the two of brothers next door with jars of momma's delicious apple butter. She always canned large amounts and different varieties of homemade canned foods in Mason jars and stocked them up on shelves in the basement. Momma had so much of everything that she didn't even miss the jars that were taken.

It was in the winter of 1968 and I was still living on the corner of Thirteenth and Highland Avenue, attending Park High school when, "My world suddenly came to a complete halt." The worst thing that could've happen, happened! I was pregnant at the age of seventeen, and still in high school. My baby's daddy, who I met while I was in school, came visiting the school he graduated from several years earlier. We dated for a little while, and then suddenly, he was gone. I felt abandoned, very hurt, upset and embarrassed. I was pregnant and not married, having a child out of wedlock. The pain of hurting and disappointing my parents was heart wrenching. Me, their eldest daughter, the one they had so much trust in, failed them. At my weakest, I succumb to the pressure that inevitably changed the course of my life. I had plans and dreams to accomplish, and having children was one of them, but not then, not before I graduated from high school and finished my career.

When I was in junior high school I enjoyed performing in little skits and talent shows. My classmates and I enjoyed singing (pantomime) and pretended we were Diana Ross and the Supremes, Martha & the Vandellas or some of the other female vocalists and groups. On a couple occasions we even performed as the Beatles. My teacher and audience always enjoyed our performances. I even took drama class when I was in high school and did well. My drama teacher was very nice and fun, he and my classmates were so encouraging and supportive of me. They often told me I was good in class. I enjoyed singing and acting. If I didn't volunteer to do anything, my teacher delegated me to do something. Raisin in the Sun and Romeo and Juliet were two of the most fun and entertaining of the plays we performed. We did well and had a total blast acting our parts. There was not a dull moment in my drama class, it was truly a fun class.

My first career choice was to be an actress a "movie star" because I loved seeing and feeling the enjoyment of people, when I capture their attention and stir their emotions, allowing them to escape for just a little while, the reality of some of the burdens and frustrations that life throw at us. Being able to preoccupy my audience's attention and allowing them to embrace the message with a favorable feedback like, "It was exactly what I needed and well worth my time" from my audience. I truly enjoyed expressing myself through entertaining, by providing people with a temporary means of escape, enjoyment.

My second career choice was to be a loving and caring nurse. Because of the lengthy childhood illness and positive caring experience during my hospitalization as a patient, being a nurse allows me to give back, to be able to emulate the love, care and compassion for my patients the way the nurses and other hospital staff cared for me. I wanted to give back to the world and make a positive difference in lives of people!"

It was Saturday in June, the month of the big event, the wedding of my friend next door. She and her fiancé were getting married. They were an exceptionally nice-looking couple. Lots of family and friends were present and the wedding was simply wonderful. After the marriage ceremony was over, the wedding party stayed around taking lots of photos and afterwards went out driving around the city honking their horns and enjoying the festive occasion.

A little while later, after driving around the city, the bridal party returned to the hall. The big moment came when all of us young single ladies were standing to catch the bridal bouquet. At first, I was not going to participate in trying to catch the bouquet, but my friend's family encouraged me to, so of course I did. The bouquet was tossed, and I, the six-month pregnant young lady caught the bouquet. But the strangest thing about it was, I really didn't try to catch it. The bouquet was tossed directly to me and I caught it. Strange huh!

My friend's new husband was home on a leave for his wedding and spent a little time with his new bride and family then went back to make plans for his bride to join him later. She was still living next door with her parents. We were still spending lots of time together. One day she really pulled one over on me. She coordinated a surprise baby shower for me. My sister and momma helped her out. I was shocked and couldn't see how they could've planned it without me finding out. My friend really planned it well. She didn't act or do anything out of the normal. One Saturday afternoon I went with my friend visiting her grandmother who lived around the block from us. I went with her often to visit her grandmother. They were a real close knitted family. They never made me feel badly or ashamed of being pregnant and unmarried. They all made me feel like part of the family.

When we came from visiting with my friend's grandmother, my friend came home with me. When I entered my house it suddenly got noisy. My friends and family came up to me laughing and caressing me. The house was all decorated with pretty baby décor'. We ate, played games and had lots of fun. I received so many nice gifts and things for my baby that I couldn't hardly find room to put everything. I had already bought a few things for my baby but after the baby shower, I had lots more. I was so grateful to everyone for thinking enough of my baby and me to plan us such a beautiful baby shower. It was so special, and much appreciated! An event I'd never forget.

With the coming of my baby, my parents saw the need for our family to purchase and move into a larger house. It was late summer, and I was entering the final trimester of my pregnancy when we moved back to the north side into a two-family upper and lower flat, located on the corner of Kewaunee and Superior Street.

My older brother, sister and I lived in the upper apartment. My younger brother, the one that was always a thorn in our side, a pain in the butt, when we were younger, had already moved out. Yeah! Thankfully, he finally grew-up. My parents and baby brother lived downstairs from us. We had three bedrooms upstairs and three bedrooms' downstairs. To have more bedrooms we converted the large dining room into a big roomy bedroom for my baby and me. Our house sat upon a slight hill on the corner of Kewaunee and Superior Street. It had plenty yard space and a beautiful large open front porch, which everybody adored. Our neighbors were also property owners who took good care of their property.

We're settled into our new home and my due date was rapidly approaching. The doctor's visits were coming more often. Although I was getting bigger, I was still very active, even turning cartwheels in our big back yard. I loved turning cartwheels. Momma eventually asked me to stop turning cartwheels, and of course I stopped!

It was my doctors' appointment day and I was outside helping momma, as per usual, with hanging out the laundry on the clothe lines, while waiting for my sister's boyfriend to come from work to drive me to my ninth month OB/GYN appointment. My sister was going along for the ride. Her boyfriend soon drove up, he had a friend from work with him. The four of us left for my appointment. My sister and I sat in the back seat and her boyfriend's friend, sat up in the front seat with him.

My doctor was very pleased that my baby and I were doing so well but ordered a routine prenatal blood test to check my blood type before giving birth to my baby, that could've been at any time.

My blood test, the blood factor was Rh-negative, a rare blood type. Because of the results I had to receive an intramuscular injection of RhoGAM, an immune globulin after the birth of my baby and future babies to prevent my Rh-negative antibodies from destroying my baby's Rh-positive blood cells, that could cause very serious complication and even death to my unborn infant.

Time came for me to give birth. It was my first try or experience at this thing called child birthing, and I could already see it was not going to be fun, a picnic. The contractions, the labor pains started coming a couple hours after supper. I wasn't sure if it was a cramping stomachache or what, but as the evening went on the pain and discomfort worsened and forced me to go downstairs to momma for her help. Momma, being more familiar with this child birthing thing, wasn't at all overly concerned, or thinking my baby was quickly about to make his/her grand entrance. Momma was observing me and trying to help me keep up with my contractions while tears were beginning to flow. Momma told me to go back upstairs for my suitcase that I already had packed to take with me to the hospital. I did as she asked. While I was upstairs for my things, momma had already awakened daddy to take us to the hospital. My sister stayed downstairs with our baby brother, and my parents and I took off for the hospital. I really was not at all a sissy or wimp, but the continual intensifying pain was more than I could ever expect a human being to have to endure. I would not have ever in all the days of my life thought bringing a precious innocent little baby into the world would be so painful and what made it even worst, the pelvic checks. It seemed as if time stopped, was going nowhere. I was in labor, agony for fourteen hours; an eternity, *at least it felt like it, ouch!*

Yes, it finally happened after many hours, I gave birth to a 7 lb. 14 oz., 21" healthy precious little boy. My sister gave my little bundle of joy his first name, and I gave him his middle name, which is my oldest brother's first name. Both my baby and I survived the labor and delivery without complications. It happened again! Another one of life's important events that my pediatrician told my momma several years ago, when I was younger and stricken with a serious childhood illness; I would never be able to "bear children," and lead a normal life, *happened!* By the Love, Grace and Will of God, I lived to carry and deliver a full-term healthy baby boy. **Praise the Lord!**

CHAPTER 7

Returned to School after Giving Birth

School was already in process when I had my baby and after having him, I had to remain out of school until after our six-week checkup with my OB/GYN. Although I had to wait for those six weeks to go to school, the first few weeks I was able to receive home tutoring and for the last three weeks I went to my tutor's home to be taught.

My tutor was nice and very helpful. She was very encouraging. She made me feel very proud that I did not allow getting pregnant to stop me from completing high school. I told her how determined I was to graduate with my senior class. I also shared with my tutor, how much momma was so helpful and a blessing with taking care of my baby while I was trying to finish school.

My six-week checkup went well, and I was finally able to go to school, which was a different high school from the one I went to on the south side for my first two years. When we moved over to the north side, I had to change schools, which was a good distance to walk; from the corner of Kewaunee and Superior St., to Horlick High on Rapids Dr. The best thing about the long walk, was smelling all the delicious aromas that came from O & H Bakery. *Yummy!*

After moving on the north side, I entered my senior year late at Horlick High and the classes had already started. The classes I originally registered for were at Park High, so I ended-up having to change a couple of classes. Thankfully, with the credits I already had from Park and the classes that I was taking at Horlick, gave me more than enough credits to graduate with my senior class.

I kept my grades up and school was going well. Having momma at home taking care of my baby while I was at school made it much easier for me to learn, not having to worry about him. But the downside was, I had no time after school, to be involved in programs or socialize with my classmates because I had to hurry home to my little guy.

At three months old, my little guy was already the king of the house. All the attention was on him, and my baby brother felt a little ignored, especially by me. Although he was my younger brother, I treated him as if he was my own child. We were very close. I spent lots of time with him before I had my baby. In fact, some of the people in our neighborhood probably thought my brother was my child because when they saw me, they usually saw us together.

The initial pain and disappointment of my teenage pregnancy had been replaced by the deep love and care they had for their very first grandchild. My parents were proud that I did not use my teenage pregnancy as an excuse to drop out of school. They were very loving, caring and supportive of my baby and me. I was so blessed, thankful and appreciative, to have such wonderful parents like them.

CHAPTER 8

Introduced to My Sister's Boyfriend's Friend

One of my friends from Park High who lived on the south side visited my baby and me on the weekends. She was a year ahead of me and had already graduated. Because we looked so much alike, we were often mistaken for sisters.

My girlfriend continued to visit on the weekends, spending time with my little guy and me. We looked forward to the weekends listening and dancing to all our favorite songs on the record player, sitting around talking, laughing and playing with my little guy. My sister, who was pregnant with her baby, waited on Saturdays for her boyfriend to come over, and they'd go out to eat and shop.

Well it was as usual a Saturday afternoon my girlfriend was over visiting my little guy and me, and a little while after she arrived, my sister's friend also came over for his regular weekend visit. But this one particular visit, my sister's friend brought his buddy from work with him, the guy that was in the car with him before, when he came to give me a ride to my last prenatal visit. Well any way, my sister's friend invited him to come along with him, to visit me. He told him he thought I was a nice person and he wanted him to meet me, that I had had my baby, and we were both doing well.

Ever since that Saturday, my sister's boyfriend's friend began to visit often, but that Saturday was the first time we had seen one another since I had my baby, over three months earlier. I introduced him to my girlfriend who was visiting me and my baby. After introducing them, I took my sister's friend's friend to see my new little one sleeping in his crib. Looking down at him smiling, he said he was a handsome little guy. That was the first of many positive visits my little guy and I received from my new male friend. He visited weekly, on Saturdays along with my sister's boyfriend. He took me out to eat and go shopping for my baby and me. My girlfriend liked my new friend and thought he'd be good for me. My girlfriend's visits became less frequent, but we kept in contact with one another.

As time went by, my male friend began to spend more and more time with my baby and me. His feelings for my baby was getting stronger. He treated him as if he was his child. Every week after he got his check, he took us shopping to buy him a new outfit to wear. My little guy's closet and drawers were full of lots of nice clothes. We, along with my sister, her boyfriend and other family members also took lots of photos on the weekends. When I wasn't in the photo, which I really preferred not to be. I was usually the photographer, shooting the pics and everyone thought I did a pretty nice job at it.

My sister and her boyfriend along with the two of us went on lots of double dates. She was the one that kept all the fun going, she was such a big jokester, who really kept us entertained especially when things really got to be boring. My sister was so much like daddy, the life of the party. While we were out for the evening, momma took care of my little guy for me. He was such a good baby. He was always so happy and content.

My friend and I spent lots of time talking. He shared with me his reasons and plans for being in Racine. He was originally from the south, in Mississippi and moved up north for the summer break to work for an older brother who had his own landscaping business, but fortunately, he also landed a part-time job working for Racine Park & Recreation.

He received a scholarship to a college in Mississippi for his singing. He had a nice bass voice. His chorus director in high school encouraged him to apply for a scholarship, which he did, and was accepted. But he first wanted to earn a little money before leaving for college. While living in Racine, he was living with one of his nephew's and his wife, the son of his older brother

"I'm Glad *You* Know Me!"

and wife, who he lived with when he was down south from the age of fifteen to eighteen, after leaving from the care of his grandmother and aunt, and until after he graduated from high school. My friend's nephew and wife did not have any children. It was only the two of them, but I thought it was very nice of them to accept him into their home. When I met my friend's nephew and his wife, it seemed as though we had known one another for all along, we immediately bonded.

My new friend also had an older sister, the only girl of all his six siblings on his dad's side. She and several other relatives of his moved from Mississippi to Racine. He also had seven other sisters and three brothers on his mother's side, a total of eleven children with my friend being the youngest of all the siblings on both, his mother and father side of his family. Most of my friend's siblings on his mother's side of the family remained down south.

My friend lost both his parents when he was very young, his mother when he was just two years old and his father when he was ten. After the death of his mother and before the death of his father, he lived between his father and other older family members. His father later died from a tragic automobile accident and went to live with his grandmother, his father's mother and aunt. At the age of fifteen my friend moved in with his older brother and wife. A year after moving in with his brother, he lost his grandmother, and his aunt soon moved to Florida to live with her only son.

My heart ached just listening to my friend's life, sad misfortunes. I felt so sorry for him; not having his mother and father in his life, and even worst, at such young and tender ages. My friend was a little shy, but he was a wonderful, loving and gentle person. He always remembered what his daddy's mother, his grandmother told him when he was just a little boy, after losing both his parents, "You lost your parents at such a young age but God did not leave you alone, you're special and chosen by God, he loves you, He's your Father."

CHAPTER 9

Proposed to While Still in High School

I t's December nineteen sixty-eight and my friend was still in Racine living with his nephew and his wife. As often as he could when he wasn't working, he spent lots of time with my little guy and me. He ended up not leaving for college after all. My friend lost the desire and motivation to attend college. He remained in Racine working, and to be with my little guy and me. He was such a wonderful kindhearted person, who would do anything for my baby and me. I was very blessed that my friend and my parents got along well with one another.

With my friend losing both his parents when he was younger, it helped him to appreciate the special relationship he and my parents shared. Losing his parents and being raised by good close relatives who loved him, helped him to turn out to be a very nice and loving guy. My friend also had a nice sense of humor. He loved to joke and have fun. That was something he and my family really had in common. My siblings and extended family liked and accepted him with open arms. I am thankful to God for my sister and her boyfriend who were instrumental in our getting to know one another.

After several months of dating and building a close and loving relationship, my friend was ready to cement our relationship. The special moment came, and my friend proposed to me, yes, while still in high school, my friend asked me to marry him. I was very surprised. He had grown to love and be very close to my little guy. It was so hard for me to grasp the reality of him even wanting to marry me, someone who already had a child, and it wasn't even his.

Of course, my response to my friend's marriage proposal was **an *absolute* yes!** I was truly in love with him and he continually proved his love for both my baby and me. Besides, I already had a partial family anyway, having him in our lives would only complete our loving family unit. My fiancé didn't want to set the date too far off, so we began discussing our wedding plans, but the actual wedding date could not be determined yet, because I was still in high school and had to plan well, to avoid being kicked-out of school and miss graduating with my class.

Earlier in our dating, I made my fiancé totally aware of the situation between my baby's father and me. Later, his older sister asked him, only out of concern for her younger brother, about my baby's father, because she did not want to see him hurt, or experience problems dealing with my baby's father. My fiancé told his sister he loved both of us very much and was willing to take the risk in order to have us, rather than not try, and lose us. He also said to his sister he was very confident that everything would work out, that he would work very hard to be a good father and husband.

The following Saturday afternoon, when my fiancé came to visit, he told me what daddy said to him, imitating daddy's facial expression, with a slight smile on his face; "I heard it supposed to be a wedding around here, but nobody's asked me". My fiancé said daddy appeared sort of strange at first, but then they both broke-out laughing very heartily. After their big laugh, my fiancé said he asked daddy's permission for my hand in marriage. That was just the beginning for my daddy, it gets better! My fiancée said, daddy chuckled first and said to him, "So you're ready to break your neck huh?" Yes, again they laughed out heartily. When my fiancé told me all that daddy said, I even laughed out heartily myself, but that's my daddy, a big jokester; a very exciting and fun-loving person. I was so glad my fiancé had already found that out about daddy; his great sense of humor.

After discussing and changing our wedding date several times, we decided to get married next year in the spring, in May, a couple weeks before I graduated from high school. We didn't want to wait and put it off any longer than we had to, so we went ahead and planned the special day next year on May 24th. We were pretty sure some people would think I was pregnant again because we were getting married so quickly, but we knew better and really wasn't concerned about what people thought.

Since I was still be in school, we agreed to keep our marriage quiet, and to keep it small and simple. We planned to get married downtown at the Racine County Courthouse, with a few family and friends as witnesses. A couple weeks later, after graduation, we would have a small nice reception, using both my upstairs apartment and my parent's the lower level.

My fiancé said he felt badly about the way we were getting married, that I deserved to have a big nice formal wedding. He promised me if we were still together in twenty-five years, for our twenty-fifth, 'Silver Anniversary', he would make it up to me. We would go all out and do it right, and do it big-time. I thought that was so sweet of him, but it wasn't really a big deal to me. I was just so excited about us getting married.

The problem was, once I was married, my position as a student would change, so I had to be secretly married during the last couple weeks of school, because if it was found out, I could've possibly being expelled from school, and that would have been a terrible nightmare. All the time and work I had put into school and end up being kicked out, not having the opportunity to graduate with my class, I couldn't take that chance. I also had to plan for my senior prom next year.

My fiancé was working second shift and requested off for my senior prom. He bought and put on lay-away one of the most beautiful elegant one of a kind long black formal evening gown made from crepe fabric that conformed nicely to my body and had a nice low neck line with an oval shape cluster of Rhine- stone sequences that sat atop of gathered fabric starting just below the center of the breast line that flared upward and down the length of the gown. It had a long sheer flaring black trains on each shoulder. It was one of the most beautiful elegant evening gowns I had ever seen. My fiancé liked it as much or more than I did, he really liked it a lot. He also bought me the most gorgeous pair of shoes and other accessories to go with my gown, for my big day!

CHAPTER 10

Married, Senior Prom, and Graduation in '69

The big day finally came Saturday, May 24, 1969 a beautiful sunny Saturday morning and we were getting married, everyone made it to the courthouse on time. Daddy, my sister's friend, my soon to be husband's sister and his nephew were all there. The marriage ceremony conducted by the judge was short and sweet. It happened in a few minutes and we were married and immediately became a family of three.

Who would have ever believed, not even a year ago earlier in June '68, when I was in my second trimester of pregnancy and caught my friend's wedding bouquet that I would be getting married, not even a year later? It gets better, to a guy I didn't even know a year earlier. What do you think about that?

I was married and life was good. My family and I continued to live in the upper flat where I lived prior to getting married but we were renting from my parents. My brother moved out and my sister and her little baby girl moved downstairs with my parents and our younger brother. My family had the entire upper flat to us. My husband was a good provider and continued to work the pm shift every night. He was so good to my little guy. He enjoyed playing hide and seek and other little children games with him. They were truly bonding well.

The big event, Senior Prom night was quickly approaching. I made my final payment and picked-up my dress from layaway. I also had my new shoes and other accessories. I was all ready for my big day, to step out in my beautiful breath-taking elegant evening gown; secretly married, on Prom night, Friday. I was so excited; but the excitement came to a sudden disappointment.

The Thursday evening before prom night, my husband called from work to tell me he wouldn't be able to take me to my prom. His voice sounded so sad. He was upset that he had to disappoint me. He said his supervisor told him they could not find anyone to work in his place. I did not make a big deal of it because I could hear from the tone of his voice, he felt very badly about it. He even told me he wouldn't feel badly if I went with one of my classmates. He was so considerate, because he knew how much I was looking forward to my senior prom, my special, long anticipated event. I told my husband not to worry or feel badly about it, it would be ok if I didn't go to my prom, because I was still excited and enjoying being a newlywed, just getting married a couple weeks earlier the thrill of being a wife was quite new and exciting. The saddest thing was, I never had the opportunity to wear my gorgeous, elegant, one of a kind evening gowns. It truly was beautiful and unique!

Although I missed my senior prom, all wasn't a total loss. I was already married, and I still had my graduation ceremony and wedding reception to look forward to; two more very special events.

The day of my graduation ceremony went well. My husband and several other family members attended. Their presence and support made me feel special. We all went out to eat afterwards and had a wonderful time. Momma stayed home with my little guy.

Saturday evening, two weeks later, after graduating from high school I was celebrating another very important event in my life; my wedding reception, which was postponed until after graduation, as planned. The evening did not start out very well at all. It was thundering and lightning and raining down cats and dogs. I was beginning to get nervous because it had been raining for several hours. I was so afraid that no one would show up because of the rainstorm, but after a little while, the guests started pouring in, despite the bad weather.

After a little while, it finally stopped raining, cleared up and the sun came out. I was so thankful that it stopped raining because I invited so many wonderful and special guests; family, former classmates and friends from Park, and some of my classmates from Horlick, as well as one of my favorite teachers from Horlick. My former boss and his wife from a summer job program that I worked a couple years earlier while attending Park, also came. I was so excited, happy and very thrilled that my grandmother, Momma Eula and a very close and dear family friend came all the way up from New Albany, Mississippi to attend my wedding reception. They made me feel so very special. Momma Eula made her special and everyone's favorite lime-flavored frothy punch. One of her secrets, it had vanilla ice cream in it. It was the most delicious tasting punch that most of us ever had. The punch was the topic of the entire evening. Momma Eula also brought my beautiful graduation gift with her. It was a hand-stitched, multi-colored king-size quilt. She made it with alternating fabric shapes and beautiful Christmas colors; red, green and white. It was so obvious that Momma Eula put lots of love, time and energy in stitching my beautiful holiday quilt. She must've started stitching it while I was in kindergarten. I really love, adore and appreciate my beautiful quilt, which I still have until this very day.

My wedding reception was going well, and everyone were enjoying themselves; talking, eating and laughing with one another. I separated my guests; the mature guests were socializing downstairs in my parent's home and my age relatives, friends and classmates from both schools, were upstairs in my apartment. Some of my guests were not friends with one another but they thought enough of me, our relationship to ignore their feelings about one another, and attend my wedding reception. I thought that was very nice and considerate of them to push their feelings aside, to make my occasion special and I was so appreciative to them for it. My husband and I was so happy that everyone came and enjoyed themselves. We were very attentive to our guests, going back and forth, up and down the stairs, socializing with everyone.

My guests began to inquire about why I kept my marriage such a big secret for the last couple weeks. I told them I had to keep it quiet because, I didn't think I would have been allowed to remain in school, and if they knew I was married, I could've gotten kicked out of school and missed my graduation. Therefore, I had to be careful, because, if there was an accidental slip of the tongue, which could've easily happened, and it would have been all over for me. I was very determined to graduate with my Senior Class of '69". Yes, indeed, my small postponed wedding reception turned out to be *fantastic!* All the guests enjoyed themselves tremendously and raved about all the good food, which was "homemade" and cooked by momma and my grandmother. How about that? My wedding reception was so nice, it couldn't have been any better if it had been on the same day of my wedding. I received lots of beautiful gifts, cards, wonderful words of encouragement, and memories that will last me for an entire lifetime.

Our marriage was going well after several weeks. My husband and little guy became inseparable, they loved each other and truly enjoyed their times together. Others viewed their relationship as that of a loving father and son, which lead my husband into wanting to make it legal, he asked my permission to be my son's father; to adopt him as his own. I was so surprised that I really didn't know how to respond, except, *you do?* I really sort of already knew but I asked him, why? He said he loved my son very much and wanted to be his father, giving him his name. He also said we were a family and he wanted all of us to share the same name, because he grew up in a family who had several different last names. I understood and appreciated him for such a kind and unselfish request, for thinking, loving and caring so much for my son enough to want to adopt him and give him his name. I did not have to think very long or hard about that decision at all. After all, he was the only male in our lives since my baby's birth.

After hearing about the adoption, my husband's older sister that lived in town, once again shared her concern for him having problems with my baby's biological father. My husband told his sister he never saw or met my little guy's father, and never gave thought of him challenging the adoption. He also said he was willing to take a chance and go through with the adoption, taking things as they came. After their discussion, my husband's sister seemingly understood, and was supportive of his decision.

I understood, as an older sibling myself, her concern for her brother's safety and wellbeing. His sister only wanted the best for him, which was perfectly understandable.

My husband's decision to adopt my son was quite clear and final. We scheduled and went to see our adoption attorney, which was also my parent's attorney. We were sitting in his office; my husband was sitting beside me with my son on his lap, a happy and healthy little eight months old boy, receiving lots of tender loving care. The attorney was very friendly and seemed to be pleased with what he was observing. He first started asking me about my child's biological father. I told him I didn't know where his father was and that he had not been in our lives. He continued to ask questions while observing us. He first asked how well we got along as a couple, then as parents and as a family. He seemed to be very positive and accepting of our responses.

After our long conversation and discussion with our attorney, he commented on how well my son and husband got along. I told him that I met my husband when I was in the final trimester of my pregnancy, that my son probably thought he was already his father, because of him being in his life so early in his life. Our attorney commented that he could see my husband being his father and thought my husband would be a good father and provider for my son. He went on to say my husband must really love and care a lot for my son for him to want to adopt him, giving him his name. That comment immediately brought a conversation back to mind, what my husband had said earlier about having everyone in his household with the same last name.

Once our attorney was finished speaking and observing us, he brought out adoption papers, explained them to us, allowing us ample time to read over the information and sign our signatures. He informed us that we would receive a phone call in about four to six weeks, after all the papers had been reviewed and approved, finalizing the adoption. We would have to return to sign "our" son's new birth certificate that would later be mailed to us. We both felt the appointment went very well but the waiting time brought with it much anticipation.

The time finally came. We received the call from my attorney's office, that the adoption had been approved and we had to go to his office to sign my son's birth certificate with his new last name. My husband and I were so thrilled and excited about the wonderful news. It was a very important and cherished moment for *our completed family.*

CHAPTER 11

Announcement of New Addition to our Family ... Sad News of Husband's Draft into the Army

We were a couple months into our marriage and family life was going well, so well that we were about to have a new addition to our family. Yes, I was expecting another precious little baby. We were not really planning on having another child so soon after getting married, but it happened. We were going to love it just the same, besides, our little guy would have himself a little playmate.

In early August, my husband received a phone call from the nephew he lived with before we were married, informing him he had some mail in a large envelope for him that was sent to his house from his sister who lived down south, saying, "The mail must be pretty important because his sister had never sent mail to his house for my husband before". After hearing that, my husband immediately left and went to his nephew's house for his mail.

As soon as my husband picked-up his mail, he saw that it was from the Department of Selective Services Office in Mississippi, and immediately opened it. It was a letter ordering him to report to the Department of Selective Services Office. The correspondence provided him with a telephone number to reply to, informing them of his current residence. My husband was shocked after reading the letter and shared the news with his nephew and his wife. After leaving them, he entered the house with a sad look on his face, handing me the letter to read. I couldn't believe what I was reading. I was in shock. We both were in complete disbelief and, not knowing for sure of what was going on, didn't feel right to either of us. We were just married, less than six months earlier, we were still newlyweds.

The following Monday morning before going to work pm shift, my husband made a call to the Department of Selective Services in response to the letter and to inform them that he no longer lived in Mississippi but had moved to Wisconsin. They ordered him to report to the Selective Services office in Racine. He reported to the Selective Services and was given orders to go to Milwaukee in two weeks for testing, and for a complete physical. By then we were beginning to get nervous. I guess I was kind of naïve or just plan in denial with what was going on. I reassured my husband that I didn't think Selective Services would draft him into the military because we were expecting and had an infant in diapers.

The two weeks were up. My husband went to Milwaukee for his physical, and about a couple weeks later he received a letter, informing him, that he had passed the physical and was accepted into the U.S. Army. Hearing that sad horrifying news turned our world completely upside down, and adding to that, another couple weeks later he received a letter ordering him to return to Milwaukee to be sworn into the army. We were absolutely devastated. We had our little crying spell but once we got ourselves calmed down, we went downstairs to tell my parents and family the sad news. No one could believe what they were hearing. They were saying, this can't be true, y'all just got married, have a baby and another one on the way, how can this be happening?

Everyone was so sad and disappointed by the news, but what could we do? nothing! My husband was drafted into the U.S. Army and had to report to Fort Campbell, KY for his basic training in a month, on September 7, and after basic training he had to go for further advance training (AIT) in Fort Knox, KY. Training for the job that he would be doing while he's in the army, his Military Occupational Service (MOS). He would also find out where he would he be going to serve the remaining of his military time.

I was already sad because I was pregnant and my husband having to leave and go into the military, what made it worst, we were basically still newlyweds and he was leaving us in the same month of our son's first birthday, before he became a year old this month on the 24th. His daddy, playmate, and buddy, the one our little guy enjoyed playing hide-and-seek with, will soon be leaving us. The sad thing was he was so young and had no idea what was about to happen, crushing his fragile little world.

My husband felt confident and glad that he was leaving his family in the good hands, and safety of my dear loving parents. Having them living downstairs from us helped him to feel even better about leaving us, especially with me being pregnant with our second child.

Time was flying by so quickly and the days were getting shorter and shorter. The very thought of my husband leaving us deeply grieved my heart.

Early Sunday a.m., September 7th had come, and it was time for my husband to leave for basic training to Fort Campbell. We were both very sad and tearful. Daddy dropped him off at the bus station downtown to leave for Milwaukee, where a group of them were meeting together to go to Fort Campbell, Kentucky for basic training. I stayed home with our little guy who was still in his bed sleeping. After seeing my husband off, I went back to bed and cried myself off to sleep.

A little while later our little guy awakened and started his day as per usual, looking for his daddy. My husband's morning routine was to play hide-and-go-seek with his energetic little guy. As soon as my husband heard him getting out of bed; his cute little footsteps running towards our bedroom, my husband jumped out of bed and quickly hid from him. Well this morning wasn't any different than the others, so at least that's what our little guy thought. He climbed out of his bed running to our bedroom to see his daddy, but his daddy was not in bed, so he and began looking for him. He looked and looked, calling for his daddy. He went into all the rooms including our large walk-in pantry, off from the kitchen. I was in the back of our apartment, crying softly, not wanting him to hear me.

Finally, after our little guy wasn't getting anywhere trying to find his dad, he became very desperate. Crying, he went into the kitchen and pulled a chair up in front of the door leaving from our apartment down to my parents, and stood himself up on the chair, unlocked the door and went downstairs, crying, and looking for his daddy, but he couldn't find him down there either. So, he came back upstairs, still crying and asking for his daddy, my baby wanted to know so badly, where his daddy was. Trying to hold back the tears, I swept my little guy up into my arms, ran into my bedroom and fell on my bed. We both cried ourselves off to sleep. Our hearts were truly crushed. Our, 'finally completed family' suddenly experienced a major void, 'the absence of a wonderful husband, and an amazing father'!

CHAPTER 12

The Celebration of Our Little Guy's First Birthday

We celebrated our little guy's first birthday, September 24, the end of the same month that my husband, his daddy left for the military. We had to celebrate our son's birthday without his daddy. It was somewhat of a sad occasion, not having him around to celebrate it with us, but it truly was a blessing to have our little guy alive and healthy, to see his first birthday.

Time passed slowly while my husband was in the army. I only received letters from him a couple times a week because they spent lots of long tiring hours in training and had a limitation on writing letters until after they were finished with basic training. I wrote him often and enjoyed receiving his letters. He always reminded me of how very grateful and appreciative he was to my parents for taking such good care of our little guy and me while he was away. He thought so much of them. Momma included us when she prepared meals for her family. I sometimes helped to prepare meals, we switched-up and prepared each other's favorite dishes. When I was a little girl, Momma enjoyed cooking for us. Lucky for me, I was never fussy about what she cooked. I usually liked whatever I was eating. Momma enjoyed watching me eat. She was an excellent cook and baker; therefore, it wasn't hard for me to enjoy my food.

I enjoyed preparing one of my daddy's favorite dishes; fried beef liver smothered in dark brown gravy with sweetened buttery rice and hot biscuits. He always went on and on about that meal. Daddy enjoyed it so much, he once said to me, "Phyllis, It's something about your liver, rice and gravy." To hear that coming from daddy made me feel good, because I learned how to cook it from watching momma while she was preparing it. Obviously, I must've really mastered the art of cooking his fried beef liver smothered in gravy and rice, because he really enjoyed those meals a lot.

Oh well, then again, I guess you can say daddy had another favorite food he really liked a lot. Yes, I was back into making him "Wimpy" again, when he wanted his hamburgers, but as for paying me on "Tuesday", well, I wouldn't even think of it. His gesture was his cute and funny way of convincing us girls, my sister and me into making him hamburgers. Daddy truly loved his cheeseburgers.

My parents were so very wonderful to us, I couldn't ever repay them for all they were doing for my family and me. They were awesome, loving and caring parents and I thank God so very much for them. The rest of my family were also very concerned about our wellbeing. My little guy enjoyed playing with his uncle, my youngest brother and his first cousin, my sister's daughter. He was fun loving, smart and an energetic little boy. Momma gave him his nick name *'Bam Bam', after a cartoon character in* The Flintstone's, *little rough and energetic boy, and that, my guy truly was!*

Time passed, and I finally got a call from my husband. I was so happy and excited to hear from him. He called me with some good and not so good, terrible news. He had finished with basic training and AIT and would be coming home for the weekend in mid-November, and back again in December for the holidays with family. But after the holidays in January, he would be deployed to Viet Nam. At that very moment I had a big lump in my throat. I couldn't believe what I was hearing. He, my new husband, couldn't be going there, not now into an active war zone, leaving us; our son, unborn child and me. I was devastated, but I didn't want him to hear it in my voice. I quickly got off the subject, telling him how glad I was to hear from him and how I couldn't hardly wait to see him.

My husband was bringing one of his army buddies' home with him in November for the weekend. His friend and family lived in California and he didn't have the finances or time to fly home for such a short stay, for only a couple days, and return by Monday. My kind and loving husband invited his buddy to come home with him. He didn't want him to be left alone and the rest of their unit gone to be with their families. The small group of them left driving from Ft. Knox, Kentucky to Wisconsin.

My husband and his friend arrived home Friday evening just before dusk. We were so happy to see one another. Our son was so excited and happy when he saw his daddy. He hadn't forgotten him at all. He ran to him, and his daddy swept him up into his arms, and they hugged and kissed one another.

After eating a nice filling dinner momma prepared for the evening, along with a scrumptious homemade dessert; pound cake with vanilla ice cream. We spent the rest of the evening going through family photos, listening to records, laughing and talking, enjoying one another's company until everyone became tired and ready for bed.

Early the next morning my husband's friend awakened me with the wonderful aroma of a nice hot breakfast and all the trimmings. He really did it up. His friend was serving me, his friend's wife breakfast in bed. Much to my surprise, I found out later my husband was jealous. He didn't like the fact that his friend was giving me all that special attention and he wasn't. Guess what, his friend didn't even care about my husband being upset. He knew my husband would soon get over it. Although his friend did not look his age, twenty-five, he was six years older than my husband, but had often been mistaken to be a lot younger than he appeared.

Because the big jokester my husband was, he had lots of fun joking with his friend about his "little boy" face, because he didn't look his age. My husband was only nineteen years old, but they both looked to be around the same age, so his friend had both age and experience in knowing how to please a lady, especially a pregnant one, as I was. After all, he was also married and had a wife and family in California.

Later that evening, they prepared dinner, a full course meal; southern fried chicken, mashed potatoes with brown gravy and green peas with nice buttery dinner rolls and sweetened iced tea. The entire meal was superb! I could've easily gotten used to all the pampering and attention. Our little guy had a super appetite and ate everything on his plate. For dessert we had a slice of pound cake and ice cream, left over from the evening before. My husband and his army buddy were thrilled and proud that we enjoyed the meal so much. The meal simply said it all. To top it off, the guys did the dishes and left the kitchen nice and clean, maybe even better than I would've. Wow!

After a couple hours of socializing, laughing and listening to music, my husband asked me if it would be okay with me for him and his buddy to step out for a couple hours to visit with his older brother in town. How could I be so selfish and not want them to go out and have a nice visit with his brother, especially since they had been so wonderful to me. After thinking about it, I thought it was a good idea for him to visit with his brother before returning to Ft. Knox, Kentucky.

The weekend was wrapping up quickly and time went fast. Sunday afternoon came and it was time for my husband and his army friends to return to Ft. Knox, Kentucky. Their ride came for them, but before leaving, my husband's friend asked us if he could be our unborn child's God Father. We both were shocked. I didn't quite know what to say. I looked at my husband and he looked back at me, smiling and nodding, as if saying yes, and we both excitedly replied, "Yes!" I further replied, "Of course you can, I'm surprised you even asked." My husband's friend was so thrilled. He hugged me and shook my husband's hands. We were also thrilled. They both kissed and hugged us, and off they went, heading back to Ft. Knox, Kentucky. I was saddened to see my husband leave, but happy for the quality time we shared together, and eagerly looking forward to his return in December, when we can spend our holiday's together as a family before leaving for deployment to Viet Nam.

CHAPTER 13

Husband Comes Home Before Deployment to VietNam

It was a couple days before Christmas and my husband was dropped off by one of his army buddies who lived up in Milwaukee. We all were happy to see him, and he was just as happy to see us. After kissing, hugging and saying our hellos, and spending a little time with family, my family of three went upstairs to our apartment and enjoyed the remaining of the evening together. I did not want my husband to worry, so I waited until he came home to tell him about a situation that had finally been resolved; the army not sending my monthly allotment checks for several months, putting me behind on a couple of my bills. I was very blessed to have my wonderful parents as my landlords because I probably would have been evicted if I had been renting from someone else. I told my husband, once my checks started, they came regularly.

Christmas with family was wonderful. We had all different varieties of tasty foods, and the most delicious desserts you could've ever eaten. Momma made most of the dishes and all her traditional holiday desserts, with some help from my sister and me. You could smell the delicious aromas of food from outside. Yummy!

After completing our meal, we socialized, laughed, and had fun conversing about the past. My brother, the former nuisance, the one closest to my age, entertained the family playing on the piano. He really set the holiday in a nice festive mood; playing and singing beautiful Christmas carols. He also played a few of his favorite R&B and Jazz songs. He was good, quite entertaining. Some of us kidding around, attempted to play the piano but could not measure up to my brother. Momma didn't do too badly for herself. She played some of her favorite songs; "I'm Going to Take a Sentimental Journey". She played another song that we never really knew the title of, but it had a nice beat and rhythm, and was easy to pick-up on and learn.

Gift exchanging was fun and exciting. Everyone seemed to really like what they received. I received one gift that was especially important to me, because daddy bought it for me, which I thought was special for a father to buy his daughter. Daddy bought me the most beautiful two-piece maternity outfit. It was the colors of Christmas. The top was a pretty green, with three-quarter length cuffed sleeves and a pair of matching multi-colored; red, white and green tweed slacks. Of course, momma helped daddy pick out my beautiful outfit. They both liked it a lot themselves. It was gorgeous, and immediately became my favorite outfit. Everyone else thought it was nice too.

My husband's time home with family really went fast. It seemed as if he had just come home, and he was already getting ready to leave again. But before leaving, our family went to a photography studio and had family pictures taken. Of course, I wore my favorite, beautiful gift; the two-piece slack outfit daddy bought me for Christmas. Our family of three 'and-a-half' were matching very nicely. The photographer did a nice job with our family pictures, and we were very pleased with how they turned out.

The next Saturday evening was going to be the last Saturday my husband had to spend with us before getting ready to be deployed to Viet Nam. Realizing that, I planned a couples evening out with our family; a group of five couples. One of the couples, my sister and her fiancé were planning their wedding for next year in December. But sadly, my husband won't be able to attend, he will be just finishing-up his time in Viet Nam.

It was our last Saturday evening together as family and as couples. We drove up to a nice Night Club in Milwaukee. The music was soft and soothing. The other couples were enjoying themselves; listening to the music, laughing, conversing and drinking, but my husband and I were very quiet, sad and down hearted; in a melancholy mood. The very thought of my loving husband going off into a dangerous war area, and so very far away from us, his family, deeply grieved our hearts. The soft music even intensified our sadness, causing us to become tearful. The other couples noticed and began to be tearful. We appreciated them so much for wanting to spend that special time with my husband and I before his deployment. Most of my husband's remaining time at home with us, his family was sad and tearful.

It was a week later, early Saturday morning, January 3rd, and I rode with daddy to drive my husband to Milwaukee's airport on his way for deployment to Viet Nam. We left our little guy in bed sleeping, and in the safe and loving care of momma, his wonderful grandma.

Seeing my husband off was more painful than I could've ever imagined. I cried all the way back home. When we arrived home, my little guy was already awake, and again, asking and looking for his daddy. Crying, I swept him up into my arms and ran upstairs to my apartment, thinking, how in the world can I tell him, my precious little guy who wouldn't even understand; his daddy was gone?

My baby, the 'bun in the oven' and I were doing well. I was getting fatter and fatter from all of momma's good cooking. My baby was healthy and very active. It felt as if he/she was playing tackle football inside of me. I was hoping for a sweet little baby girl, but if it was another boy that would've been fine too, I was still going to love him just the same. The most important thing was that my baby was healthy. When I was younger, I said if I ever had children, I wanted to have two, one of each sex, with the boy being the oldest to take care of his little sister, siblings.

Well time passed and it had been quite a little while since I heard from my husband. I hadn't received any letters or any responses from the letters I sent to him. I knew he was busy and in the forward area (combat area) and his days were very long and busy, but I thought it was strange that I had not heard anything from him. Much to my shockingly surprise, I later found out my husband had been injured and hospitalized, for which he was later awarded a Purple Heart Medal.

My delivery month was April and only two months away. The thought of my husband, my baby's father not even being here to witness the birth of our unborn child, saddened me, but I was being kept plenty busy; taking care of my little guy, going places and doing things with momma, my sister, sisters-in-law and some of my friends. They all kept me very busy, which gave me less time to think and worry about my husband, it also helped time to go by faster. We had fun socializing; shopping, eating out, and playing our favorite table games like; Bingo, Pokeno, Monopoly, Pity Pat and Tonk, a card game. Momma and I also spent time putting together large beautiful scenic puzzles, and when we finished them, we glued them on pre-measured cardboard, framed them and hung them on the wall. They were beautiful!

CHAPTER 14

Family Welcomes the Birth of Our Precious Baby Girl

It was early on Tuesday morning, April 14th when I gave birth to a beautiful healthy plump baby girl. The labor was just that, long, painful and laborious. I was so glad to have that part over, but my little baby girl seemed really irritated about leaving her warm snuggly haven into this cold world. She was crying so hard when she was placed in her crib that she pushed herself over onto her back. Everyone in the room got such a big laugh from it. When photos were taken of her, I asked if they would take an extra one for me to send to my husband, they were very nice and did what I asked of them. The photo of my sweet little baby was so cute, but she was crying so hard.

Momma and my sister were anxiously waiting out in the waiting area to hear the wonderful news and see our new addition to the family. After my baby and I were cleaned-up they were able to come in and visit with us briefly. They were excited and happy that my baby was a healthy little girl. They really laughed when I told them about her crying so hard that she pushed herself off her stomach over unto her back. Everyone agreed that she probably didn't want to be disturbed and brought out from her warm, toasty and comfortable abode into a cold and unfamiliar place. We agreed that my husband would be proud when he heard the wonderful news of the birth of our precious little baby girl. My precious little baby and I had a long rough night and it was early in the morning, we were totally worn out, and my little baby was already fast asleep in her crib, and I was beginning to fall asleep on my family. They quietly left us resting.

The second of what wasn't supposed to happen, happened, me not being able to bear children according to my pediatrician's knowledge. Yes, God not only blessed me to have one, but two; a second healthy child. I lived through another full-term, healthy pregnancy. We must conclude once again, the power of My loving father, God has defied the limited knowledge of man.

My husband flew home on furlough after finishing his tour in Viet Nam, and before going to spend his last six months, still out of the states, but in Germany.

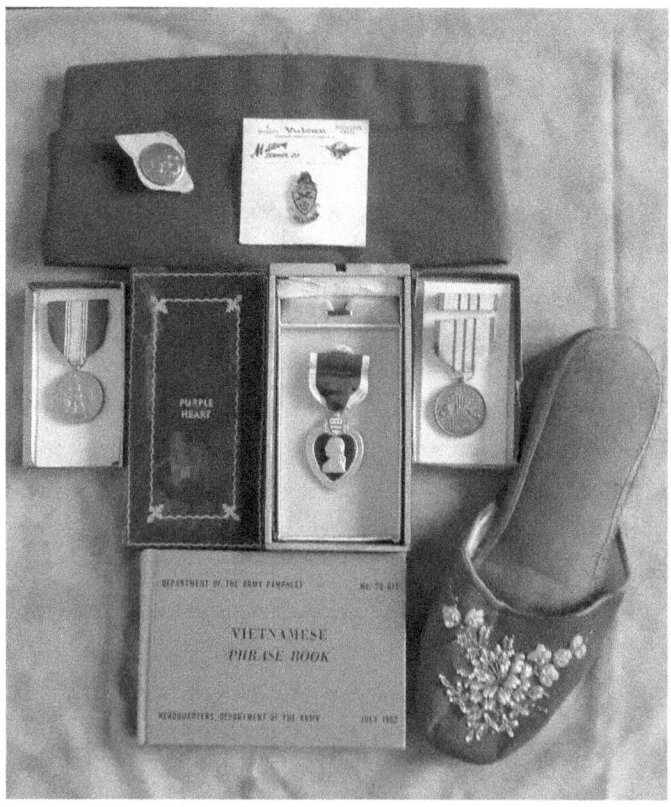

Although the Viet Nam war wasn't where my husband wanted to be; but as souvenirs, and because he liked them too, he brought a beautiful emerald green satin lounging jacket and a beautiful pair of hot pink slippers home to me. They were wonderful gifts, souvenirs, and memorabilia.

My husband was just seeing his little baby girl for the very first time. He was so glad to see us all, but especially his baby girl. She was eight months old, and just as cute and plump as she could be, but the strangest thing was, she would be playful and content for a while and then began to be irritable and cry. During those spells, she would cry, and cry, even when she was full and dry. Momma said I probably marked her; passed my crying off, onto my baby because I cried so much while I was pregnant with her. And after thinking about it, I realized I did cry quite a bit while I was pregnant, during the sad and terrible time when my husband was drafted into the military and going to Viet Nam, leaving our little guy and me pregnant, behind when we were newly married.

My husband's army buddy from California later flew in to visit with his new goddaughter for the weekend before they were off to Germany. This was also his first time seeing her. He was so happy and excited to see her. He has three boys of his own, but no girls. She seemed special to him. He kissed her and held her so tightly in his arms. He brought her an adorable outfit that his wife helped to pick out, along with a cute little cuddly stuffed animal. He also brought our little guy a cute little red truck which he really enjoyed playing with it. He absolutely cherished his little red truck.

During the time my husband and his buddy was home they did not discuss their Viet Nam experience. They enjoyed one another, being with family and friends laughing, joking, listening to music on the record player and playing games. My husband and his friend brought home a new card game they learned to play while in Viet Nam called Spades. They said after work, they sometimes played all night especially if they didn't have to work the following day. Spades was a fun game they really enjoyed playing because it helped them to relax, unwind and forget where they were, even if it was only for a little while.

CHAPTER 15

My Baby Girl Had A Bad Ear Infection

This furlough for my husband was no different than the others. It went by so awfully fast. We were never without something to do or somewhere to go, but I was concerned that our baby girl was not always a happy little girl. One minute she would be happy and playful and suddenly began to cry, grabbing at the side of her face. I searched her entire body, from the top of her head to the bottom of her feet and could not find anything wrong, no diaper rash or sores or anything. She wouldn't be hungry or soiled but she continued to cry. We all felt so badly for her, but we just didn't know what to do for her. Those episodes continued throughout my husband's furlough at home. I was beginning to see that her crying so much, which he was not at all used to, was beginning to bother him.

Early Monday morning came, my sister and I road along with my sister's husband who drove my husband and his buddy to Mitchell Field airport in Milwaukee departing to Germany. Where they will be spending their final six months in the army. Momma was home taking care of our babies. This departure was sad but not nearly as sad as all the previous ones, because I knew that was going to be the last time, I will have to say good-bye to my husband. Although we'll have both the good and not so good memories of the time he spent in the military; Viet Nam, those memories helped us to appreciate the strength of our love and marital relationship, and looking forward to all the future years; once again, we'll share as a complete family.

My sister and brother-in-law dropped me off, home from the airport and as I was entering the house, the very first voice I heard was my baby crying. Momma was holding her in her arms, singing and walking with her trying to console her and stop her from crying. She had been crying all morning since she woke-up. Momma changed her diaper and tried to feed her, but she wouldn't eat. She was back at grabbing at the side of her face again. I was really concerned about my baby, so I immediately called for a doctor's appointment. I was grateful to be able to take her in to be seen that day at an afternoon appointment.

Well I found out my poor, poor, precious little baby girl was suffering from a bad ear infection all along. I felt so terrible that I waited so long before taking her to the doctor. My poor, poor little angel was in so much pain, which was why she cried so much and was so rest broken. It all made perfect sense, her grabbing at the side of her face while she was crying. Her doctor treated her with ear drops and an oral antibiotic. Her initial dose of antibiotic was in the form of an intramuscular injection (shot) into her fat little thigh. Boy, did she ever bellow, my baby did not like that at all! I felt so badly for her, I even cried myself. I had to put ear drops in her ears several times a day and give her the medicine (antibiotic) from a syringe into her mouth until it was all taken. Our little sweetheart truly didn't want to have the ear drops or the medicine. When it was time for her medicine, I always had to get momma's help and boy did we ever have a fight on our hands every time. She truly was one stout little sista!

My husband called and I told him why our little lady was crying so much while he was home on furlough before going off to Germany. He felt sad, very badly for her. I told him with all the business and activities going on and with the excitement of him being home, our baby's symptoms slipped by us. Momma said she was thinking our little princess might have been crying so much because I cried a lot while carrying her. We could already see a difference in her after a few days on her medicine. She seemed to be a much happier and satisfied baby. Yes, we all were relieved to find out what was wrong with our little princess. As time went on, she wanted to be more independent and became more curious with her surroundings.

"I'm Glad *You* Know Me!"

My little lady began to be very determined and did not give up very easily when she became bored playing with her toys on the floor. If she really wanted something and after having had her eyes fixed on it, she tried and went for it.

Turning back the hands of time and recognizing my little princess' determination; at birth, when she was placed lying on her stomach into her crib beside me, crying, she pushed herself off her stomach over onto her back. My baby had so much determination!

Months later, while my little lady was down on the floor playing with her toys, she saw something she wanted and began pulling herself up onto her feet, grasping onto chairs and other furniture in her path to get to the object she wanted and started walking from then on. I guess my little princess must have been thinking she had lots of catching-up to do since dealing with her illness, bad ear infection, and didn't have time to go through all the small stuff, preliminaries. She simply cut right to the chase. The phrase, "You have to crawl before you walk" simply did not apply to my little lady. She was truly unique, her own class act!

A few years later I entered my children into a Children's Photo Club called Peter Pan. The studio came to our home to take photos of them for birthdays and special occasions. One time the photographer convinced me into sitting in a photo with my children. It was a nice photo, but I wasn't really into having pictures taken of me. I preferred more being the photographer, shooting the photos.

CHAPTER 16

Bad Sewage Forced Us Out!

In the spring of 1971, my children and I were forced out of our apartment from living upstairs, and renting from my parents and moved into a two-bedroom upper apartment on the south side of town, on Twelfth Street. We lived upstairs from my landlord, six months before my husband was due to come home from the army, for good! Living with my parents on Kewaunee and Superior St., since before my husband and I were married, made it very difficult for me to move. But because of the bad and on-going sewage problem, which daddy hired plumbers several times to fix, ended-up being temporary fixes, and the problem always returned, causing blockage and back-up of the sewage, throwing off a terrible sewage odor, that circulated throughout the entire house, up and downstairs.

My parents also had to move. They moved on the southside as well. We loved and had lots of good and bad memories, living in our house on Kewaunee and Superior, but my parents did not want to put any more money in trying to fix the major problem of the large tree and deep roots in our back yard, that had grown down into the sewer line, causing lots of back-up and blockage problems. I was especially saddened to have to leave all the good times and many wonderful memories. It was where I met my husband, finished high school, married my lifetime mate, had two beautiful healthy babies and learned how to drive my first vehicle. I'm sure

I've probably missed some other important events and details, but those are just the few that comes to mind.

Living in our new apartment upstairs from my landlord was going well. They were a nice family with two children, a girl and a boy just like us, but the girl was quite a few years older than her brother. They were very mannerly children. My landlord liked having me as their tenant because I took good care of the apartment, kept it nice and clean. They especially liked that my children were nice and very well behaved. We lived there for about a year after my husband came home from the military. After working at J. I Case Co. for about a year or so in 1972, we bought and purchased our first home on Virginia Street, and the following year my parents moved in the same neighborhood, on the same side of the street, only three houses north of us.

CHAPTER 17

My Painful Experiences in the Workplace

Later on after several months of moving into our first home, I started my first adult job working at Lincoln Village Convalescence Center (LVCC), working as a nurse's aide, a long-term care facility for the sick and elderly recovering from their illness. It was located on Byrd Avenue, approximately a three-minute drive from where I lived, on Virginia Street. Momma and her two younger sisters enjoyed their work very much as nurse's aides, working at Lincoln Lutheran Home (LLH), a long-term care, geriatric facility on the north side. They encouraged and inspired me to become a nurse's aide.

Momma worked part-time second shift with one of her sisters, and her other sister, the youngest, worked full-time, third shift, 'the graveyard shift'. Momma and her sisters often had long conversations on the phone talking about their special experiences with their resident's and families. Listening to their conversations, along with them talking with me about the fulfillment they received; the type of work they did, convinced me into going into that field of work, taking care of the elderly and the sick. It really shouldn't have been a surprise that momma and her sisters had a love for caring for others, their momma, my loving grandmother, Momma Eula was a nurse mid-wife when they were younger, growing up in the south. Momma

Eula brought hundreds of babies into the world, both black and white. She was liked and very well known by the families in her community.

After I was hired at my new job working part-time, second shift, I arranged and set-up a sitter for our children; a school age teenage girl who lived across the street from us, to sit with them for about an hour a day after I left for work until my husband came home from work.

The first evening of work, I went through orientation and was introduced to the residence, staff and my co-workers. Everyone was friendly, but one co-worker sort of stuck out. She seemed to be a nice person, but I noticed later after we gave cares, finished charting on our residents and were waiting to do bed check; the last cares for the night. She was off to herself and not talking or holding a conversation with anyone. During that time the rest of us enjoyed conversing quietly while time was passing, until bed check, and before going home for the night. My co-worker reminded me so much of when I was younger and going through a serious illness, being restricted from physical activity and having to sit off from my classmates while they were at play. I was often sad about having to sit off to the side, and away from them, not being able to participate in physical activities with them. Seeing my co-worker sitting off to the side rekindled those sad memories. I didn't like seeing her setting alone.

It was convenient for my first couple days of work at my new job happened to land on momma's days off. She was my transportation to my new job.

Well, the earlier part of the second evening at work went well until after supper but when we were getting our residents ready for bed, the evening progressed to be not so nice at all, in fact, it very easily could have been my last night, because I felt like I had been severely misinformed about my job. I was so upset with my momma and aunts for talking me into doing that kind of work. It was a very busy and chaotic night. I ended up having to clean up bowel movement off just about every other resident. It was absolutely the worst thing I had ever experienced. At the end of the evening I felt dirty and worn-out, not to mention, betrayed! I couldn't believe my momma and aunts would set me up the way they did. I was so upset and disappointed. As I was leaving for home at the end of the shift, I was quietly thinking, "I'll never come back here again!"

"I'm Glad *You* Know Me!"

As soon as I walked into the house from work, I reached for the phone and called momma. When she answered the phone, I was so upset and crying telling her about my terrible night at work. As our conversation went on she managed to calm me down, telling me to not to be upset and reassured me that episodes like that didn't happen very often, it was some type of stomach or intestinal virus passing through, which actually was the case, but it didn't make me feel any better. The remaining of our conversation was on our resident's, how important we were to them and how much they and their families appreciate and depended on us. Our conversation ended on a very pleasant note, with me having a complete change of mind, 'heart' and ready to go back to work on my next scheduled day.

The next scheduled work evening was calm and went very well. I enjoyed taking care of my residents, meeting their families and working with my co-workers. It was indeed a night totally different from the second one. It didn't take long for me to find out that momma and her sisters were right about the importance of our work as nurse's aides, care givers.

After working a while, my residents looked forward to seeing me. They knew they would be well taken care of. They and their families felt the love and compassion I had caring for them. I built strong loving relationships with them and their families. It felt as if they accepted me as a part of their families. Although I had love and compassion for all my residents, there was this one resident, we bonded very well. We became so close that she gave me a special nick name, "Bright eyes", my resident said I had bright and very expressive eyes. She, along with some of the other residents were very involved in different types of activities and classes. Her interest was in ceramics and pottery classes and working with her hands. She molded a beautiful cylinder-shaped vase for me. Initially I refused to accept it because I did not want to get in trouble from accepting gifts from the residents, but she became upset that I did not accept it, so I went to my supervisor and explained the situation to her, how insistent my resident was that I accept the vase she made special for me. After our discussion, my supervisor gave me permission to accept the vase from my resident, and to this very day, I still have and cherish that vase.

My husband worked first shift and we only had one vehicle and he needed it to drive himself to work. A couple days of working, I found out I had a co-worker who passed my street, on her way to work and set-up transportation arrangement with her, to pay her every two-weeks on payday. She was a little older than me, but I really liked and looked up to her. We worked together on the same unit (hall). The transportation arrangement worked out well, "for a while".

I always made sure I was ready when my co-worker, driver came to pick me up for work. We were never late for work. When she came for me, I could see her coming from standing in front of my picture window, turning the corner onto my street, Virginia Street.

One particular day, on my way to work, as I waited for my driver to drive up; and after not seeing her turning onto my street yet! thinking, I had enough time to take a quick run to the bathroom before she came, which was a very short distance from where I was standing. As I was coming out of the bathroom, I heard a car horn honking and honking. It was her and I quickly ran out to the car. While getting into her car she said in a very harsh and piercing tone, "You just about got left!" That particular day, her husband was driving. I was so heartbroken because I had been standing and waiting patiently and decided to quickly run to the bathroom before she came, they most've turned onto my block just as soon as I walked away from the window. It was not like it took me forever, or that we were going to be late for work anyway!

After going into work that evening, everything was going well. We took report from our nurse and began to take care of our residents; it was a quiet night and our residents were finally tucked in for the night. We charted on our residents and answered their call lights until time for bed check. My co-worker who was also my driver, had one of her bad migraine headaches. I suggested to her to go home, and not to worry about staying to help with bed check, that I would get help from one of the other aides on the other unit. I also told her, to keep her from worrying about me having a way home, I would call my husband to pick me up from work. I finally convinced her that I really didn't mind her going home, I was more concerned about her. She went to tell our nurse, who, by the way was also her good friend, about her bad migraine headache and wanted to be excused for the evening. She first reported off to the charge nurse, before leaving to call for her husband to pick her up from work.

We normally worked with two nurse's aides for each unit, but since we were short a worker on our side, the three of us teamed-up and combined the units and worked together. Bed check and teamwork went very well. All our residents were nice and clean and resting comfortably. Before we knew it, we were all finished working and leaving for the evening, saying our good nights to one another. We had a great and uneventful night!

It was my next scheduled day back to work, and my driver, co-worker came to pick me up as per usual. She was smiling and said she was feeling much better since we last saw one another, a couple nights ago, when she went home early from work with one of her bad migraines. After arriving to work and getting report from our nurse, I began doing my rounds, checking on my residents; toileting them, passing out their towels, night gowns and other necessities. We also passed around pitchers of ice water to our residents. My co-worker and I alternated turns passing the ice and water pitchers, but I usually volunteered and went more often and left my co-worker, driver over on our unit passing resident's laundry or whatever. That evening I took my turn and went for the water. In order to get the water, I had to go over onto the other side of the building, where the water and ice dispenser was located. While filling the water pitchers, my co-worker, driver, came over by me. Her demeanor had changed drastically from the time I left her on our unit to fill the water pitchers. She was very upset and yelling angrily, with her hand on her hip, wagging her head; and shaking her finger saying, "I heard you were raising h__ __ _ because I went home the other night!"

She was speaking about the last evening we worked together, she was suffering with one of her bad migraine headaches. I was the one who actually encouraged her to go home, reassuring her that I would be okay without her, that my other co-workers would help me with bed check, we would work together as a team, which we did, and bed check went very well. I was shocked, totally unprepared for what I was both seeing and hearing, and before I knew it, tears were streaming down my face. My co-workers were waiting in line for water and ice, and witnessing this very shocking, traumatizing and painful moment as it was happening. They were listening and staring while I was trying to hold back the tears and explain to my driver-co-worker, trying to tell her, that I never said anything at all about her going home. While crying so hard, I tried to help her to remember, I was the one who encouraged her to go home in the first place. The hurt, pain and disappointment I experienced felt as if a semi-truck had crushed into the center of my chest. I couldn't believe what I was seeing or hearing, and especially, from whom I was hearing it. Someone I admired and looked up to had suddenly turned against me. It was absolutely devastating, the worst day of my life. I was taken so much by surprise that I did not even think to ask her who told her what I supposedly had said regarding her going home, which was *'a big fat lie'*. In fact, once my co-worker left for home that evening; her leaving wasn't even discussed or mentioned by me, or anyone else to that matter!

After the very painful, unbelievable and traumatic experience, I was so upset that I was not able to calm or settle myself down enough to finish my work. It bothered me so much that I went to the charge nurse and asked to be excused from work for the rest of the night. She could see I was hurting and in deep despair. She allowed me to leave for the rest of the evening. I immediately went to phone my husband and he immediately came for me. While riding home, I tried to explain to my husband what had just happened, but I could not stop crying long enough. He felt very sad for me, knowing I had experienced something so awfully painful and traumatizing.

My first experience in the workplace as an adult, co-worker and friend had suddenly been turned upside down. It showed me a totally different side of a person that I thought shared a mutual relationship, but obviously didn't! After the painful experience, my husband no longer wanted me to depend on my co-worker for transportation. He decided, until things changed, he could find another way to work and let me keep the car, and he would catch a ride with our brother-in-law.

Although my husband and brother-in-law worked for the same company, they worked in different departments and one or the other sometimes had to go in earlier or work over-time. Thankfully, when momma wasn't working, she was usually helpful with giving me a ride. We were living only three houses from one another, made it very convenient for us. Another choice, back-up plan I had for transportation was to catch a ride from one of my other co-workers, someone I would pay and would not be taken out of their way.

After the painful and terrifying experience in the workplace, I continued working as usual; working with my co-worker, former driver, treating her no differently than I did before, attempting to honor the Golden Rule, *"Doing onto others as I would have them do unto me."*

"I'm Glad *You* Know Me!"

One evening while working with another one of my co-workers I asked for a ride home. I told her how close I lived from work, and that I would pay her for the ride. She said she had to first check with her husband, because he was her transportation. My co-worker went ahead and phoned her husband, saying he would give me a ride home.

Well the evening was far spent, we had completed our shift, and everyone were leaving for the evening, saying their goodnights and heading out to their cars. My co-worker and I walked out together to her car. Her husband was parked next to the curb near the employee entrance. My co-worker was starting to get into the front seat beside her husband. As I was reaching for the rear passenger door, a large dark vicious looking dog jumped up in the back seat of the car, staring and growling ferociously at me, exposing his long, sharp fangs. I immediately pulled my hand back, and obviously refused the ride from them. In shock and trying to do all I could to hold back the tears, I ran back inside the building and phoned my husband to pick me up from work.

It happened once again, I went through another very terrifying and traumatizing experience, 'painful relationship in the workplace'. It was one of the most hateful and meanest things anyone could ever do to someone. It was not as if I was afraid of dogs or anything at all, my family were avid animal lovers. I even had my own personal pets. Obviously, my co-worker and her husband did not really want to give me a ride after all, but they did not have enough decency to at least try to fake it. Her husband did not have to bring their ferocious, mean looking dog along with him; to frighten me into not wanting a ride from them. Well it worked!

It wasn't even like, my co-worker's husband, driving me home was taking them out of their way. Besides, I was willing to pay him for the ride. On their way home, they had to pass my street, which was only a couple minutes from work. I really didn't think I needed to get my husband out of bed to pick me up, especially with him having to be up an extra hour earlier for work the next morning. Another terrible incident was witnessed by my co-workers at my workplace.

After the mean and hateful experience of the incident with my co-worker's dog, which was witnessed by my other co-workers who began to be very distant with her and treated her differently; without friendly conversations, and kept their relationship strictly work related. Subsequently, my co-worker inevitably felt ignored, slighted and decided she no longer wanted to work with us.

I continued to work for approximately three more years, and later went on to pursue my passion as a loving, caring and compassionate nurse!

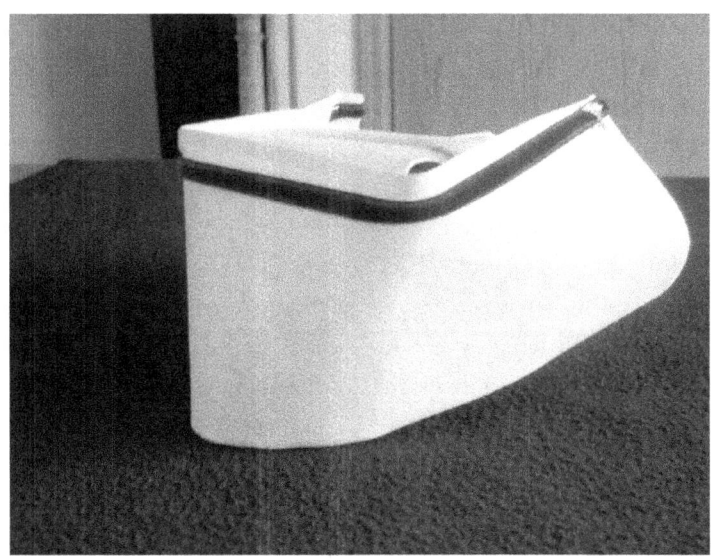

CHAPTER 18

My Passion Left Me Broken!

Because of the love and compassion I had for caring for others, which was largely attributed to the type of loving care and compassion I received as a young child, seriously ill and hospitalized for an extended period of time, *I wanted to give back!*

After much thought, consideration and many discussions, my husband and I agreed that I needed to pursue my dream, my passion, which was caring for others, and making a difference in other's lives by returning to school; college for nursing. But since we had young school age children that were very active in school activities, my husband and I decided I would only attend college on part-time basis and be involved with them and their schooling. Subsequently, I resigned from my job, and went on and registered for the Licensed Practical Nurse (LPN) program in Kenosha, Wisconsin at Gateway Technical College (GTC) and was accepted.

Before starting college, my husband and I planned for our family to go down south to Mississippi for our summer vacation. My husband had two weeks off from his job and we had enough time to visit both of our families. We first went to visit his older brother and his wife. It was the very first time I had the pleasure of meeting them. My husband and his brother were so glad to see one another. They were very close, caressing one another and playfully horsing around. His family was very nice and friendly. My husband's sister-in-law was a great cook. She prepared the best homemade fried hot apple pies, which was one of my husband's favorites. It felt as if I had known his family for a long time. We had a mutual fondness right away, a relationship I was looking forward to only get stronger as time went by.

After leaving my husband's family, who lived further south, we headed on our way up to New Albany where my grandparents, and great grandmother lived. Much to our surprise, as we were driving up onto their property, there were all kinds of cars parked all over, and as we were getting out of our car, we heard lots of laughing and talking. Amazingly enough, we found out, momma and all her siblings from Racine were visiting my grandparents, their parents at the same time. Surprisingly, my husband and I had no idea that momma, daddy, and all momma's siblings and their families from Racine had planned on going down south on vacation at the same time. We were shocked about how things turned out. But once we started thinking about it, we figured, well, most of the guys worked at the same place, J.I. Case Co. and were on vacation from work, so why not go and visit their parents and grandparents? What was so nice and convenient, some of my relatives had parents and grandparents, from the other side of their family who lived in the same area, just up the road from my grandparents, giving them an opportunity to spend time with both sides of their family.

All my grandparent's grandchildren and great grandchildren had themselves a blast running back and forth from my grandparent's popular neighborhood store, which was located next door to their house. It was there, where we first tasted Jumbo pies (Moon Pies), Nehi, assorted fruit flavored soda pops, Dr. Pepper Sodas, Orange flavored push-ups, Old-Fashioned Coconut Bars, and lots more yummy treats! As a matter of fact, it was Momma Eula and Popa Robert's neighborhood store where daddy was first introduced to peanut brittle candy. He really liked that candy a lot, but it didn't seem to like him very much. The candy was so hard, it caused him to break and lose some of his false teeth, which he probably swallowed a few.

Momma Eula's excellent cooking, along with a little help from her girls, was so very scrumptious. One of our favorite meals was fried chicken with all the fixings. The delicious fried chicken came from my grandparent's large chicken coop in their back yard. When momma Eula opened the coop to take chickens out for our meal, some of the chickens escaped wondering around and had the children screaming and running all over the yard. It was quite a funny sight to see, very entertaining!

Our vacation was so much fun. We enjoyed visiting and sharing quality time with our families. We had an amazing time, but time came, and we were heading back home to Racine. Momma and daddy were also leaving with us.

Although our vacation was exciting and full of fun, I was worn out. All the socializing and activities with our families, along with not getting much rest, and resting comfortably in my own bed, left me totally exhausted!

As we traveled down the long highway, daddy and my husband were taking turns passing up one another. Daddy had a heavy foot, he did not like my husband to pass him-up on the highway and found himself being pulled over by a highway patrol officer. Thankfully, the officer was nice. He did not give him a ticket, only a warning to slow it down.

Obviously, momma had not been sleeping very much since we left my grandparents. Momma, looking over into the car at me smiling said, "Every time I look over at y'all, you were sleeping." Daddy said momma had not been sleeping, other than taking little cat naps. As I began to think, to my surmise; momma unconsciously did not allow herself to fall soundly off to sleep while traveling the highway; because of a past experience she had when she was eight months pregnant with me, 'a bun in the oven' a little over a couple decades earlier, when our family friend came along to help with the long drive up north, fell asleep behind the wheel and we scarcely avoided a horrific head-on highway collision, a near death encounter that would have left no survivors. Momma obviously never forgot that very terrifying experience!

Our family had a fantastic time on our vacation, we were back home, and I was ready to begin college, to pursue my passion. I was ready to enter the LPN program. After completing the course and graduating, my plans were to work for five years, gaining lots of work experience and later return to college and receive an associate degree in Nursing (ADN)) program as a Registered Nurse, and continue to go on even further to broaden my horizon.

On our first day of orientation, we incoming students were given a pretty lengthy and thorough outlook on all the expectations of the nursing program. It was going to be a very fast paced, involved course. Taking lots of personal and family time from us. Because of all the time and demands of the program, sadly, but some students went through divorces.

Well I guess you probably can say, I really didn't fully understand the extent of what they were saying in orientation about the strong demands of the nursing program. Going back to school almost a decade later, after graduating from high school, being married and having a family, I found out it was more than just a notion. Yes, after a while I could clearly see it was no way that I could have continued to work, take care of my husband and family, and attend college, *even part-time!*

The beginning of the first semester was quite challenging. I had to learn how to develop and sustain good study habits. After about six years later, a husband and family, I guess I had kind of forgotten how to study, but it didn't take me very long at all to catch on to what I needed to do to be on top of things. I bought index cards, took good notes, bought myself a tape recorder and even got involved in small study groups, with one of my cousins and a couple of our classmates. We worked well together and did well in our classes. Before I knew it, classes were over, and I passed first semester with flying colors. By the way, I had one of the hardest and strictest nursing instructors for my first semester clinical rotation. She was very encouraging and supportive. She noticed right away, the love and passion I had for caring for the sick. I earned good grades and lots of positive feedback from her regarding my performance in direct patient care; activities of daily living (ADLs), patient charting, patient care plans, medication administration cards, and other clinical skills and performances I needed to pass-off on. I also had lots of homework to do after leaving the clinical area.

My instructor's method of grading; was by signing her initials and placing a check mark beside her initials, confirming and validating her accepting and passing me on any of the selected check-off skills, tasks, or duties performed in the clinical area. She frequently added lots of positive comments and feedback when grading me. Thankfully, I passed first semester, and did very well. I enjoyed the experience and was looking forward to my second semester rotation.

Well, second semester clinical rotation did not go nearly as well. In fact, it turned out to be a very sad, depressing and traumatizing experience. The grading system was supposed to have been the same for second semester as it was for first semester, with emphasis placed in the areas of; attendance, direct patient care, patient care plans, charting, and medication administration cards.

Again, I did very well in my first semester clinicals. The problem was, my second semester instructor did not accept lots of my work in the clinical area, even when I attempted to correct the problems to her liking, which she did not even explain to me how she wanted them done. I was surprised, discouraged and disappointed, especially because, I had one of the hardest and strictest instructors for first semester, whom I earned good marks from and passed the class with flying colors, thinking; if I continued to apply myself and do as well as I did first semester, I would surely do well in my second semester. I thought my first semester instructor was preparing me to do well in my second semester clinicals, to again, pass with flying colors.

During my second semester clinicals, momma was an inpatient at the hospital where I was a student. She was a Type II Diabetic, overweight, and a heavy smoker. Complications landed her in the hospital. While there as a student, I heard a Code Blue announced over the intercom. Unbeknown to me, it was momma. I was immediately notified and went to be with her. Momma had had a heart attack. I almost lost my momma to death from a heart attack. Shortly after finding out about her, her mother, my grandmother, Momma Eula, from down south in Mississippi died around the same time momma was having a heart attack. She had been in a serious car accident and suffered a massive heart attack that she was not able to survive. I was so shocked, saddened and totally devastated about the tragic news of my grandmother, Momma Eula, and momma's heart attack, which could have also taken her, my momma away from me too! **So very sad and painful!**

We did not tell momma about the death of her mother until her condition was much improved. Because momma was so very ill and needed me, I was not able to attend my loving grandmother's funeral down south. I loved her so very much and felt very badly about not being able to go and see her for the last time, and to be with our family, but I needed to stay and be with my dear mother through her illness, who at the time needed me more.

A little while after Momma Eula's death, my grandfather, Papa Robert and Grandma Rhode, Momma Eula's mother moved up north to live with family.

Momma's very painful and traumatizing life changing event turned out to have given her a second chance in life. She shared with me an unusual experience she had while in the hospital, after having a heart attack. Momma said she had a talk with God, saying, "A voice came from behind the curtain and said to me, "Burmia, don't smoke anymore", momma replied, *"Okay, I won't!"* Momma kept her promise to God and never smoked another cigarette from that day forward. *Amazing!*

After entering my second semester class, I repeated all my previous positive clinical "skills" and study habits from first semester and gave very good and compassionate care. I was a good student, team member, and worked well with staff and other interdisciplinary teams in the hospital. Sadly though, for some reason I was placed into a very stressful and painful situation that inevitably altered the direction I had planned my life to go.

My second semester instructor was very distant and unfriendly towards me. I felt very uncomfortable vibes. She did not even try to hide her dislike for me. The negative experience as my instructor had broken my spirit, changed my outlook, It affected me so deeply that my grades and over-all schooling experience suffered. My outgoing personality had left. Our student, instructor relationship changed my positive and outgoing demeanor. I was broken and ultimately succumbed to the very stressful, depressing and traumatizing experience. Subsequently, I failed second semester clinicals. After that very negative experience I had a complete change of mind about returning to college; *"My passion left me broken!"*

After a little time passed and discussing with my husband on what I should do about returning to complete my schooling, I went ahead and returned to college to repeat second semester clinicals and did very well. My new instructor was nice, but I wasn't going to allow myself to get close to her, kept my distance. The overall experience was pretty good, but I was still broken; cautious, and guarding my feelings and emotions because of my previous painful experience. Because of it, plans of going any further into my career, was certainly not a thought!

Despite experiencing some very stressful and emotional tolls during a certain period of my nurse's training, I continued to persevere and successfully graduated from the Licensed Practical Nurse Program in December 1976, but I was not at all in a big hurry to go to take the Wisconsin Boards Nurse Exam. I wanted to be free from the painful thoughts of my past student/instructor relationship experience, study and stress, put it all off for a while to enjoy family and life; and try to take time to forget my brokenness.

While enjoying life again, I started reconnecting with a longtime friend and her new husband. She was the friend that was getting married back in June 1968, when I was six months pregnant. I was coaxed, encouraged by her loving family to go up with the other single young ladies and try to catch the bridal bouquet, so I did, and I caught it. Wow!

My friend's new husband was very nice and an excellent cook. They were a nice Christian couple and enjoyed entertaining guests in their home. They were very faithful and devoted to their local church. I was not going to any church, but sending my children along with my next-door neighbor's childrento a local community church on Sunday mornings, until after a few Sundays went by and they experienced a very sad, mean and disappointing incident from the other children on the bus on their way to church. I later found out from my children that the other children on the bus were spitting on them and calling them racist names and all while it was going on,the bus driver wasn't paying any attention to them. Needless-to-say, I felt very sad for our children and real upset and disappointed with how they were treated, and never sent them back to that church, and after that experience, I made up in my mind that when my children went to another church, we would be going together, as a family!

My friend and her husband taught and enjoyed teaching one-on-one Bible classes, in fact, I was one of their students. After having a few Bible classes with them in their home, they invited me to visit their place of Worship on Sunday mornings. I accepted their invitation and my children and I began to attend.

CHAPTER 19

My New Birth

Although I felt I had a happy marriage, a wonderful family and a good career as a nurse, it still felt, there was something missing in my life. I didn't know what it was.

Well it happened on Sunday morning, April 3, 1977 when "Route 66" was the subject of the sermon that was preached, and my heart was pricked into obeying the Gospel. After listening very attentively to the message, and being deeply engaged, I felt the message was speaking directly to me, so I immediately responded to the invitation call; accepted Jesus Christ as my Lord and Savior, by putting Him on in Baptism. I was buried into water by baptism into Christ, it was my new birth, and I was added to the Lord's church; "The church of Christ".

When I came up from the water I felt as though I was as light as a feather, as if a heavy weight had been lifted off me. The message of the sermon was dealing with the Bible consisting of 66 Books. The minister was explaining that the Bible, the Word of God gives us guidance and direction when we listen, obey and surrender to His will as we journey through our walk of faith. The sermon message was so inspiring and encouraging, and truly right on time. My dedication, love and loyalty to the Lord will be as that of the psalmist David, "I will dwell in the house of the LORD forever, Amen!" (Psalm 23).

After my baptism and the worship service was over, my children and I, along with some other members were invited for dinner at one of our faithful member's home. My new, spiritual family were very warm and loving. They accepted us and made us feel very welcomed.

One particular Sunday morning, as I was preparing for worship, my husband said to me while still lying in bed, "Do you know, today is the most segregated day of the week, the blacks are going to their church and the whites are going to theirs." It was so sad to hear, but it was very true. I felt so badly that my husband seemed bothered by it, and hearing him say it made me more conscious, or more aware of that fact, but it didn't stop me from hoping and praying that he would soon start coming to worship with us, and one day, we could worship together as a family. I prayed often that my husband would be baptized, added to the church and become very faithful in his Christian walk. My husband had a very nice base voice and loved to sing. Since he sang so well, he could probably help the other song leaders during worship service. My husband continued to encourage and support me in my Christian walk. Sometimes he also went to church with us and enjoyed the service each time he attended.

My daughter enjoyed going to church very much and learned a lot from regularly attending Sunday school and Wednesday evening Bible class. One Sunday after listening to the message preached, she told me she was ready to obey the Gospel, to be baptized. Her confession was taken, and she was baptized, added to the Lord's Church.

After my baptism, new birth in Christ I became very faithful and committed to all the church services and activities. I enjoyed going to church and taking my children with me to all the services. Our church's minister was new to our congregation. He came just a few months before I was added to the church. He commuted from Chicago twice a week as well other times for meetings and special events or whenever. Our minister was a very likable and fun person. He made everybody feel special, and met no strangers, he went to members' homes and felt right at home. Our minister and I shared the same birth month, October. His birthday was exactly one week after mine. We celebrated our birthdays together, of course my husband was invited and came along too. We had a wonderful time together, with good food and great fellowship.

"I'm Glad *You* Know Me!"

It wasn't very long before I was asked by my long-time friend and sister-in-Christ, the friend, that she and her husband taught me and were responsible for me being in the Lord. She asked me to teach Bible class to the primary grade students on Wednesday evenings, which I did and enjoyed teaching that age group. They were very smart and creative, and they loved learning and memorizing the Bible verses, especially when they knew they were going to receive some type of honor or recognition for memorizing and reciting the verses.

Several months later, and after I already had a good start working in the church, I took advantage of a course that our minister offered to the members, a twelve-week specialized training course called Fishers of Men (FOM). It taught us how to teach one on one personal evangelism, (Matthew 28:18 – 20). The course used the Search for Truth Curriculum, a series of lessons which teaches the gospel. The lessons assisted individuals in their search for Bible truths, God's written word. Because I was blessed to take and pass the course, I taught many students, many believed and obeyed the gospel, and were added to the church and became "New Babes in Christ."

My first employment after graduating from the Licensed Practical Nurse Program was at St. Mary's Medical Center (SMMC) on Spring Street here in Racine, as a graduate practical nurse until I received my Nurse's license. I then resigned and went on to work for Lincoln Lutheran Home on Prospect Street. The same facility that momma and her two sisters worked as Nurse's aides. My aunts were still working but momma no longer worked there. One of my classmates from Nursing school was just hired there and asked me to work with her. I went and applied and was hired on the spot. I worked part-time p.m shift with one of my aunts and my classmate worked full-time on third shift, the graveyard shift with my other aunt.

Through the oversight, blessing and approval of our minister, I later started a singing ministry, we went to sing hymns and spiritual songs to the nursing home residents where I worked along with two other long-term nursing facilities in our community. Not only did the residents and their families enjoy, and were uplifted by our singing, but the staff were equally moved by our singing as well, they all looked forward to our monthly return.

Our minister had gotten word that I was a nurse and asked me to be the nurse in our local congregation. I accepted his request and started off by doing blood pressure screenings, helping my church members to understand their medications and doctor's orders. I also sometimes accompanied them to their doctor's appointments. The congregation really appreciated and often complemented me on how much help I was to them. I was truly blessed that I was able to use my medical knowledge and skills to help my local church family.

Working at Lincoln Lutheran Home was an excellent learning experience, and a job I enjoyed going to, where everyone worked well together as a team. I supervised four to six nurses' aides on my unit. There was also a Charge Nurse (RN) in the building but seldom came to my unit unless I needed her. Once when she was making her rounds, she shared with me, she didn't have to come to my unit to check on me because I did my job well and was keeping my unit under control. My charge nurse wasn't worried about anything when I was working, realizing, if I really needed her, I would call for her.

CHAPTER 20

My Unexpected Pregnancy!

It was the winter of 1979 when we had the worst snowstorm that I had ever seen. We had a bad blizzard, it snowed for twenty-four hours before even stopping. It was coming down so much and accumulating so fast that the snowplows and graders couldn't keep up. They were so backed up that we didn't get our street plowed for a couple days. My husband and our oldest son went out several times to shovel the snow. My daughter and I stayed inside and kept warm and dry, but I made sure I kept plenty of hot cocoa ready for the workers. Out of curiosity I thought I would step out on the front porch, and I noticed there was no activity, no one on our block was outside, all the snow had paralyzed everything.

Although there was a blizzard, a severe snowstorm weather alert, it was strange to not see anyone or anything in motion. When my husband and son came inside to rest and warm-up, my husband and I were joking and conversing about what people were doing with the advisory that was given, to not go out unless for an extreme emergency. Laughing we agreed, saying there's probably lots of babies being made.

The following day the snow was still coming down heavily and did not seem as though it was going to be stopping anytime soon. Since the snow was still coming down very heavily, a couple hours before the start of my shift, I went and called in to work to let them know that I was not going to be able to come in, because my car was stuck up in our driveway and I could not get it out onto the street because my street had not been plowed yet, and I didn't know when or if the plow trucks and graders would get to my street. I lived on Virginia St., on a side street off 21st street, where my street intersects with, which had already been plowed. I also told them the snow graders and plow trucks were backed-up and I didn't know for sure when or if I would be able to get out onto the street to come in to work.

About an hour or so later my boss, the director of nursing (DON) called and said she would come to pick me up for work, and because the traffic was slow and backed-up, she would be leaving earlier for me. I told her I would have to walk up to the corner of my street on 21st St. to be picked-up. We agreed on the time for me to be standing at the corner when she arrived. There was no school for the children, so I quickly called for my sitter from across the street, who also was a student, to come over and sit with my children for about an hour, or until my husband came home from work.

My boss, the DON came to pick me up for work and as soon as I walked in, I found out there were lots of call-ins. The storm kept many of my co-workers from coming into work, and some of the workers had to stay over-time because they were stranded and waiting for either a ride, or until the snow settled down and were able to get to their vehicles. Thankfully, we managed to handle the night very well. Our residents received good care as per usual despite the shortage of the of the nursing staff. Some of the office personnel including my boss even pitched in to help. They were helpful and very considerate. Everyone worked well together as a team. Our resident's family visitors were very scarce, given the weather condition, it was not surprising at all and pretty much expected it.

Because of the situation we were especially thankful to have had a quiet, and uneventful evening. The residents were their usual selves and most of them were doing their normal pm activities. We, the staff were provided a nice complementary hot meal and all the hot cocoa we wanted.

Our shift was winding down and the phones were ringing off the hook, more call-ins. Some co-workers were still trapped and couldn't get off their streets, and the plow trucks and graders were still backed up. I was asked to stay over for the 3rd shift, but I had to first clear it with my husband and he was okay with me working the night shift, but I needed to be home with the children before he went in to work at seven the following morning. I told him I would catch a ride home with one of my co-workers that's done working at six a.m. My boss was very much okay with me staying until six o'clock. She just appreciated that I was staying over to help. I realized this was a situation that was beyond any of our control, and our residents really needed me. We had an uneventful night.

Life was going great; family, work and Church, not necessarily in that order, but life was great anyway! But after a while, I experienced some problems and went to see my gynecologist and found out I was pregnant. I received the shocking news, some news that I was not at all expecting. Yes, I was pregnant again, it was an unexpected pregnancy, because, I already had the two children I always wanted; one of each sex, a boy and a girl, but I became pregnant again, ten years after our last child. How could I've ever let that happen? Thinking I was being careful, but then again, my life was so busy with family, working and being so involved in most of the church activities. I guess I kind a lost track of important times and dates. I had been on and off different contraceptives and taking the pill caused me to have high blood pressure, so I had to stop taking them and started using an Intrauterine device (IUD), which obviously didn't work. *Oops!*

Well the initial shock and disappointment of my unexpected pregnancy soon passed, and I became very excited about having a brand new little one in our family. My husband and the children were excited about it too, having a little baby brother or sister in the family. It really gave us a lot to think about and look forward to, during my pregnancy. The sex of my baby was no real concern or issue at all if he or she was healthy, because my baby was going to be loved and very well taken care of anyway. The estimated delivery time was around the end of September, which was a pretty popular month for some of my family members; my eldest brother and eldest son.

Time passed and I was already into my final trimester; family, church, working part-time and pregnancy were all going very well. After passing through a lengthy period of morning sickness, life was great. It was good that I worked the pm shift, because morning sickness, with nausea and vomiting left me feeling weak and wiped out for a while before going into work. One of the older female employees from housekeeping told me I was going to have a boy because I was carrying him/her so high in my stomach. I told her about all the morning sickness and indigestion I was experiencing. She said that meant my baby was going to have lots of hair. She reassured me; she was seldom wrong with predicting the sex of the unborn child. After hearing her say that, I had lots of confidence in her prediction. After work I went home and told my husband and momma what the housekeeper said, I began thinking and planning more around my baby being a boy, which was quite alright with me, since I already had two children, one of each sex.

I went in to work my usual pm shift, received report from the first shift nurse, saying they had a quiet, and uneventful day. Everything was off to a nice start, after receiving report I gave report to the nurse's aides, received return calls from doctor's offices and began to pass my first rounds of meds. Because of the seriousness and possibility of medication errors while administering medications, I was concentrating and focusing on what I was doing instead of allowing myself to be distracted by what was going on around me.

Well time went by and I was finally finished passing meds, so I put away my med cart and was getting ready to go down on my break, but I first had to find the nurse's aides to let them know I was leaving the floor to go on my lunch break, but I didn't see any of the nurse's aides around, so I began walking down the hallway looking off into the resident's rooms, heading down to the resident's lounge but I didn't see anyone.

Not realizing the staff were in the resident's lounge standing off to the side, where I could not see them, waiting for me to enter, they suddenly jumped out in front of me, laughing and congratulating me. I was never so shocked and surprised; my co-workers secretly had planned a surprise baby shower for me, and the entire pm shift attended. They divided-up their break-time. Everyone brought a dish to pass. We had a nice variety of delicious food and desserts. I received lots of beautiful gifts, cards and money. Yes, they really pulled it over on me. I had absolutely no idea, what was going on. I thought it was so very sweet and thoughtful of them to plan such a wonderful celebration for my little one. It was an amazing surprise, one that I would never forget. After my wonderful surprise baby shower, I worked an additional month and went out on my maternity leave.

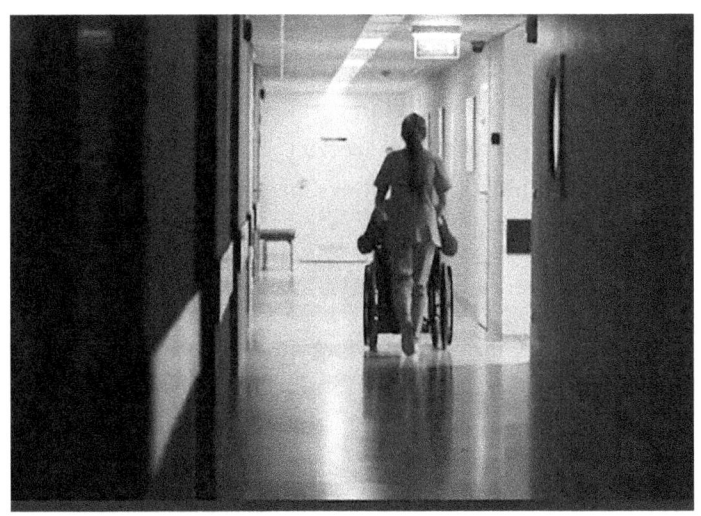

CHAPTER 21

Close Encounter of the Third Kind!

During my pregnancy leave, all momma, my sister and I did was eat and I gained more and more weight, more weight than I did with both of my prior pregnancies combined. Yes, I really enjoyed going out to eat and some of my favorite foods that I craved a lot for, were Mexican food; beefy tostadas, fried beans and rice and tacos, from a popular Mexican restaurant in town. I also loved and ate lots of healthy fresh fruits and vegetables, especially when momma cooked the delicious vegetables from her garden.

It was a Friday afternoon, momma, my sister and I went to our favorite Mexican restaurant for lunch. I had my favorite, beefy tostadas, fried beans and rice. I as usual, really enjoyed my meal. When we were done eating lunch, momma dropped me off at home. Shortly after coming home I began to have intermittent twitchy like discomfort in my lower back and stomach, but I did not let it stop me. I started preparing for my kids to come home from school and my husband from work.

On Fridays we usually went out for dinner at Burger King, our family's favorite place to go for our delicious sandwiches. My husband and I liked the whaler with cheese sandwiches, fries and milk shake, and the children enjoyed their cheeseburgers, fries and shakes.

My husband came home from work and by the time he was finished with his bath, the twitchy like discomfort had turned into real pain that was becoming more regular and intense, I was having contractions.

We were beginning to get really concerned about the increased pain and the regularity of the contractions. By this time my doctor's office was already closed for the day and weekend, but we both thought I should go to the hospital to be checked out just to be on the safe side. We did not get a chance to go out for dinner, but we dropped the children off by my parents and they took them out to eat.

Once I arrived at the hospital, I was there for several hours. They monitored me for a while, said I was having false labor pains and sent me back home. I really didn't want to go home being in so much pain, but my husband took me home. Upon arriving home, I went ahead and packed a few items to take with me when I went back to the hospital.

Later during the night, while lying in bed trying to sleeping, the contractions came more frequently and the pain more intense. They started coming one after the other like soldiers marching to a drill until I couldn't stand anymore. I was in so much pain and restless that I awakened my husband. I really did not want to go back to the hospital to be sent back home again but I could not stand the pain any longer, so my husband took me back to the hospital. As soon as we arrived, they came immediately with a wheelchair. It was obvious I was in lots of pain, so much that my husband had to do all of the talking and answering the questions. I left my husband and was taken to the labor and delivery room and examined. My cervix was dilated to 7cm and my little one was about to make its grand entrance into the world. The horrific pain from the contractions were already bad enough and having to be vaginally examined just helped to intensify the agonizing pain even more. During it all, I later found out my obstetrician was off for the weekend and an on-call OB/GYN would be delivering my baby.

While lying in bed in the labor and delivery room, I suddenly had an urge to go. I felt as if I had to go to the bathroom very badly. I asked for help and was assisted out of the bed and wheeled into the bathroom, and after being seated on the toilet an uncontrollable pressure came down, and out came blood. I was bleeding very heavily. I was hemorrhaging. Copious amount of blood was all in and around the toilet. I yelled out at the top of my voice and suddenly, I was swept up from the toilet and everything started moving very fast. My cervix would not dilate any further and my baby was in distress and couldn't come down, my baby was in real danger!

It was 2:00 Saturday morning and the entire emergency team was called in to assist with my emergency surgery. My unborn child and I, both were in danger and could die. My husband was fearful and concerned for us and had to sign a release form giving the doctor consent to perform an emergency Cesarean section to take my baby.

The entire emergency surgical team and doctor were all in place and ready to start the surgery. I was placed on my side and given very important instruction before being given an epidural, "to not move, or I could be paralyzed". I thought within myself, "As for the horrific pain that I was already experiencing, nothing short of having my head cut off could cause me to have any greater pain. I did not even as much as flinch!"

Emergency surgery was performed and was successful, from it came another healthy 7Lb. 13oz. 21inch baby boy borne into our family on early Saturday morning, September 29, 1979, and by the way, he did have a head full of the most beautiful black curly hair you've ever seen.

He, my third child; another child "I was *not supposed to be able to bear*" according to my pediatrician over two decades earlier, *happened!* Yes, once again, it was fate; God, the Holy Spirit *"watching over"* and protecting my baby and me during my very difficult and dangerous delivery; navigating my life to be used by him. Both my baby and I were truly blessed to have made it through such a terrifying near-death experience, a *"Close Encounter of the Third Kind!"* Praise be to God. It was truly evident that my loving and caring Father wasn't, and *isn't* through with me yet. That is why I can, and will openly express to you **God**, my heavenly Father, *"I'm Glad* **You** *Know Me!"*

EPILOGUE

Thank you for reading through to the final pages of this memoir. I love and am forever grateful to God, my loving Father for His power of **love** and **forgiveness,** which He exemplified over two thousand years ago, when *He gave His only begotten Son,* our loving Savior, *Jesus Christ* who himself lived a sinless life but He died for the sins of the world; yes, for me, *"My sins"* (John 3:16). I therefore, love and forgive my fellow man, God's prized creation? I am no longer broken, or in pain regarding my past unpleasant relationship experiences. Subsequently, I have been blessed with the peace of God, which surpasses all understanding. (Philippians 4:7).

Although unpleasant *'relationships'* and painful life experiences may sometimes leave us feeling hopeless alone and broken, please don't give-up; **"Love, recognize your fate and last, but certainly not least, forgive!"**

I was abundantly favored! God knew my end from my beginning. He knew me and was with me, *"watching-over"* and protecting me throughout the first twenty-nine years of my journey in life, while I was being prepared to be used by Him, for His glory, subsequently, for His prized creation **'humankind'**. Therefore, I openly and thankfully express to You God, my loving heavenly Father, *"I'm Glad **You** Know Me!"* (Psalm 139: 13-16).

Because of my experiences, I was blessed to realize God's continual presence, and my purpose in life.

Phyllis Barker-Pittman
Timeline of Events
1950-1979

APPENDIX

"I'm Glad You Know Me!"
A MEMOIR OF RELATIONSHIPS: LOVE, FATE, AND FORGIVENESS

Scriptural References

All Scriptures referenced within this book are from the

New King James Version (NKJV) of the Holy Bible

RELATIONSHIPS

Romans 12: 17-18; 13:10
Galatians 5: 14
Ephesians 4: 31- 32; 5: 1-2, 25; 6: 1-4
1 Thessalonians 5: 15
Hebrews 13: 1-2, 4-5, 16
1 Peter 4: 8
Psalm 82: 3-4; 133:1
Ecclesiastes 4: 9-10
Proverbs 13: 1, 24; 17: 6, 9, 25
Proverbs 22: 24- 25; 27: 9, 28: 27
Proverbs 31: 10-12

LOVE

Matthew 22: 37-39
Mark 12: 30-31
John 3: 16
Romans 13: 10
I Corinthians 13: 2
Galatians 5: 14
Ephesians 5: 1-2, 25
1 Peter 3: 8-9; 4: 8-10
1 John 4: 7- 12

FATE
DESTINY/PREDESTINED

Jeremiah 29: 11
Psalm 139: 1-7, 13-17
Ephesians 1: 11; 2:10; 3:20
Colossians 2: 8-10

FORGIVENESS

Matthew 6: 12-15
Mark 11:25
Luke 17: 3-4
Romans 12: 19
Ephesians 4: 31-32
Colossians 3: 12-13
1 John 1: 9

www.ingramcontent.com/pod-product-compliance
Lightning Source LLC
Chambersburg PA
CBHW071003080526
44587CB00015B/2328